Remedios

Remedios

THE HEALING LIFE OF
Eva Castellanoz

JOANNE B. MULCAHY

TRINITY UNIVERSITY PRESS
SAN ANTONIO

Trinity University Press strives to produce its books using methods and materials in an environmentally sensitive manner. We favor working with manufacturers that practice sustainable management of all natural resources, produce paper using recycled stock, and manage forests with the best possible practices for people, biodiversity, and sustainability.

This book is printed on Rolland Enviro, recycled from 100% post-consumer waste.

Published by Trinity University Press
San Antonio, Texas 78212

Photographs of Eva Castellanos on pages ii, xx, 82, and 192 courtesy of Jan Boles, Caldwell, Idaho. © Jan Boles. Photograph on page 132 courtesy of the Oregon Folklife Program. © Oregon Folklife Program.

Cover design by Nicole Hayward   Book design by BookMatters, Berkeley

⊗ The paper used in this publication meets the minimum requirements of the American National Standard for Information Sciences—Permanence of Paper for Printed Library Materials, ANSI Z39.48-1992.

Library of Congress Cataloging-in-Publication Data
Mulcahy, Joanne B., 1954–
    Remedios : the healing life of Eva Castellanoz / Joanne B. Mulcahy.
      p. cm.
    Includes bibliographical references.
    SUMMARY: "Blends creative nonfiction and ethnographic research to tell the stories of Eva Castellanoz, Mexican American curandera and community activist; explores Castellanoz's faith, indigenous identity, relationship to Catholicism, and use of traditional folk arts and healing, which she views as a way to overcome poverty, racism, disease, social inequality, and loss" —*Provided by publisher.*
    ISBN 978-1-59534-061-0 (hardcover : alk. paper)
    ISBN 978-1-59534-065-8 (pbk. : alk. paper)
    1. Castellanoz, Eva.   2. Mexican American women healers—Oregon—Nyssa—Biography.   3. Indian women healers—Oregon—Nyssa—Biography.   4. Traditional medicine—Oregon—Nyssa.   5. Mexican Americans—Oregon—Nyssa—Social conditions.   I. Title.

GN477.M85 2010
973'.0468720092—dc22   [B] 2009028401

14 13 12 11 10   5 4 3 2 1

CONTENTS

Part III. The Dream

PREFACE

To be a *curandera*, says Eva Castellanoz, is to have faith.[1] *Curan-derismo*—from *curar* (to heal)—passed to Eva from her mother, María Concepción Juárez Silva, and to both of them from God. Healing is a gift, the *curandera*, its vessel. The potential lies within, but a person must choose to develop it. Healers in many cultures are sharp-eyed visionaries at the margins; they see what others cannot. When Eva was very young, she would go each morning to the fields in the Rio Grande Valley with her father, José Loreto Fidel Silva. Gathering dew from the leaves of the squash, beans, and corn, he would anoint Eva's face. "He always wiped my eyes with the dew," she recalls. "He would say to me, 'You will see things differently.'"

Eva wants us to see differently, too, through the metaphors she crafts in everyday life, in teaching, and in healing. Perhaps she absorbed the importance of metaphor from her parents' indige-nous world, for the Aztecs believed that art "made things divine." The only real knowledge on earth could be glimpsed through *in xóchitl in cuícatl*—the Nahuatl phrase for poetry, translated as *flor y canto* or "flower and song." Life for the Aztecs was wonder-filled but fleeting: "Although it be jade, it will be broken/although it be gold, it will be crushed."[2]

Even as a child, Eva grasped this contradiction; she wanted to be a poet. As an adult, she has mastered one of poetry's central tools. Eva's metaphors evoke her own stubborn self as *la mula*; the gang members she works with as golden treasures; Catholicism as a too-tight dress; spiritual legs as the body parts that truly support us; culture as a tree with deep roots, healthy bark and limbs; faith as something beyond our measuring tools.

To understand metaphor is to go beyond logic. When Eva says that she "ties her lions back at night," we must accept that her rage at social injustice is an animal, that something can be itself and something else at the same time. We have to envision one aspect of life in terms of another. We must link separate worlds and turn the abstract into concrete aliveness. Only then can we move from blinkered vision to the wide-angle view, from illness to health, from despair to hope. Metaphor is our bridge, if we are willing to cross over it to reach new understanding. Eva's goal is nothing less than social transformation, but she begins with the simplest of movements: pressing the dew onto our eyes.

ACKNOWLEDGMENTS

I am deeply indebted to Eva Castellanoz, who gave me gifts beyond measure: faith and friendship. Her trust that I could shape a story of her life urged me forward. I dedicate this book to her remarkable spirit.

Thanks go to all the Castellanoz clan, especially Eva's children and their spouses: Diego Fidel and Cecelia (Cece) Castellanoz, Rosario Isabel (Chayo) and Ricardo Garcia, Juan Rafael (Ralph) Castellanoz, Maria de Lourdes (Maria) and Rogelio Gallegos, Enrique (Ricky) and Yolanda Castellanoz, Martin (Marty) and Priscilla (Flaca) Castellanoz, Maria Cristina (Chana) and Luis (Brown) Ramirez, Sergio (Toe), whose spirit lives on through the love and invocations of his family, and Javier (Cami) Castellanoz. They welcomed me into their lives, fed me in numerous ways on visits to Nyssa and on my trip to Pharr, Texas, and waited patiently for the completion of this book.

The support of my family and friends is bedrock. My parents, Jeanne and Paul Mulcahy, nurtured the creative pursuits of all their children. My sister Pat's support and editorial advice were essential. Many friends offered valuable commentary on

parts of the book: Judith Barrington, Judy Blankenship, Ana
Callan, Andrea Carlisle, Norma Cantú, Guadalupe Guajardo,
Ruth Gundle, Cindy Williams Gutiérrez, Kirin Narayan, Karen
Rodriguez, and Marilyn Sewell. Others buoyed my spirits with
engaged conversation: Bob Amundson, Perrin Kerns, Elinor
Langer, Scott Lyons, Bob McCarl, Paul Merchant, Holly Syl-
vester, and Sully Taylor. Special thanks go to the faculty and
staff of the Northwest Writing Institute, especially director
Kim Stafford and administrative assistant Diane McDevitt.
Their generosity created a home for my work at Lewis and
Clark College.

I am deeply indebted to the vision and encouragement of
editor Barbara Ras. Managing editor Sarah Nawrocki, always
patient as well as efficient, shepherded the manuscript with
great care. Julie Van Pelt's initial edits alerted me to critical
questions. Copyeditor Katherine Silver's keen eye and appreciation for language made *Remedios* a far better book. Thanks to
Jan Boles for his endless generosity with photos. Nancy Nusz,
Gabriella Riccardi, Carol Spellman, and Amanda Andersen of
the Oregon Folklife Program aided my research and shared my
commitment to Eva's story. Christine Marasigan, Jae Carey,
Carol Cheney, and Laura Marcus helped transcribe taped
interviews.

Institutional and financial support came from multiple sources.
The Rene Bloch Foundation financed travel to Texas in 2001.
The Espy Foundation and the Sitka Center for Art and Ecology
granted residencies in 2006 and 2007, respectively. The staff at the
Menucha Retreat Center unfailingly welcomed me. The Graduate
School of Education and Counseling of Lewis and Clark College

provided funds for research, tape transcription, technology assistance, and countless other forms of aid.

My deepest gratitude extends to my wise and patient husband Bob. He read and responded to the entire manuscript several times. His love and encouragement continue to sustain me.

A NOTE ON METHODS

This book blends creative nonfiction with ethnography—the portraits that anthropologists, folklorists, and other social scientists write. Ethnographic fieldwork relies on interviews and participant observation—observing, recording, and taking part in cultural life. Many creative nonfiction writers, particularly "immersion journalists" who spend extended periods with a person or group, use similar methods. Writers in both realms employ dialogue, scene, and other fictional techniques to engage readers. As a writer and a folklorist, I have tried to draw the most useful tools from each domain to convey Eva's experience.

The quoted material and stories of Eva's life come from interviews conducted in Portland and Nyssa, Oregon, between 1992 and 2008, and on a trip to Pharr, Texas, in 2001. I taped twenty-one interviews; at other times, I wrote notes on our extended conversations. I kept journals while doing fieldwork in Oregon and Texas and during visits to Eva's birthplace of Valle de Santiago in 2005 and 2006. Both trips to Mexico revealed local historical materials unavailable in the United States. Those visits also gave me a feeling for Eva's early years. Though Eva is bilingual and we taped interviews in English, I studied Spanish over a ten-year period. This enabled me to read primary documents in Spanish and deepen my understanding of her life. In the text, Spanish words that might be unfamiliar to readers are italicized. Accents appear in some names and not others according to the individual's spelling preferences.

The structure of the book is episodic rather than chronological; it is organized around our time together in different locations. My intention is to invite readers into Eva's casita in Nyssa, to her childhood home in South Texas, and to the Owyhee Mountains in eastern Oregon. At times, I merged into one story material Eva told me in different interviews. For example, Eva repeatedly described how she died when she gave birth to her ninth child, Cami, and was "called" to healing (a story that appears in chapter 9). Most of the short segments that open each chapter as epigraphs reappear in the text; I repeat Eva's words for emphasis and to show the context from which they emerged. I kept Eva's speech as close to the taped material as possible, occasionally changing verb tenses and other elements of grammar for clarity. I hope these methods help animate Eva's humor, lively use of language, and storytelling gifts.

Citations and endnotes suggest avenues for further exploration of Latino history in the Northwest, *curanderismo*, Mexican American religious practices, and other topics that surface in Eva's stories. These references are partial and never offered as substitutes for Eva's *testimonio*, which stands on its own.

INTRODUCTION

In July 2003, as the sun falls over the Snake River, I sit with Eva Castellanoz on her back patio. Heat lingers past dusk in Nyssa, a predominantly Latino town on the Oregon-Idaho border.[1] Eva wears jeans and a Mexican blouse embroidered with pink and sky-blue flowers; she seems far younger than sixty-three. Still-smooth amber skin encases her high cheekbones and angular features. "*Mira*," she points to a flash of shimmering green near the bird feeder. "The hummingbird is back!" When we see the quicksilver birds on this patio, Eva recalls my first visit fourteen years before. From this weathered picnic table, we watched a similar humming-bird. A sign of good luck, Eva said then. I didn't ask which of us luck would grace; both equally, I hoped.

On that first visit in 1989, I followed Interstate 84 from Portland through the towering walls of the Columbia Gorge, past the juniper and sage of the high desert, to eastern Oregon. Eva's house sits on the outskirts of Nyssa, past the Owyhee Beer Distributing Company. Two doors down from her house is the bright blue Rodriguez Bakery, its front wall emblazoned with "On the Oregon Trail." When I arrived that first time, she was out back on her knees, pulling weeds. She was not yet fifty. Her five-foot-four frame carried more flesh then, her hair was less gray; her smile revealed gaps in her teeth, since replaced with gleaming white implants. As Eva rose to greet me, dirt falling from her jeans, she seemed as luminous as the hummingbird.

When we met, I was director of the Oregon Folk Arts Program. Eva had just won a National Heritage Award for her *coronas*, the wax and paper floral crowns worn for special events.[2] *Coronas* are central to weddings and especially the *quinceañera*, a young Latina's fifteenth birthday celebration.

The following year, we worked together to document traditional Mexican/Latino arts in eastern Oregon. Soon after, Eva was diagnosed with cancer. Doctors predicted that she had little time left. Not only has she survived well beyond that prognosis, but she has thrived as a nationally recognized folk artist, *curandera*, and community activist. In 1992, I began recording Eva's stories. Since then, I have driven east to see her every year after the snow melts in the Blue Mountains. In spring, we sometimes drive to see the swallows' nests in the Owyhee Mountains. We haunt the "bon marchés"—Eva's term for thrift shops of all kinds. Once, we journeyed to Eva's childhood home in Texas.

Now I compete with many others for her time. National Public Radio, Oregon Public Broadcasting, and National Geographic teams have trekked to her home to produce documentaries. Students of folklore, anthropology, environmental studies, and Chicano/Latino/Hispanic studies find their way to Nyssa. We come to learn—all alike, all different in our seeking.

When I began this project, I wasn't sure that I could write about Eva. Numerous artists and scholars have followed her work, many better equipped than I to document her life. Though trained in anthropology and folklore to conduct ethnographic research, I had no expertise in Mexican or Mexican American history or culture. For years, I studied Spanish in order to do research. But above all, I labored to find the right vehicle for rendering her life stories. One way to read Eva's words and my shaping of them is as *testimonio*, an important form of storytelling in Latin American literature. *Testimonios* emerge from lives of struggle, often told to a cultural outsider. Both bear witness—the storyteller through his or her experience, the writer as transcriber and translator. This genre differs from Western autobiography. In *testimonios*, the "I" creates an identity through illuminating a broader collective. Many begin with phrases such as, "It's not only my life, it's also the testimony of my people."[3] Eva's story chronicles individual travail and triumph; it is also the narrative of many Mexican Americans in the United States.

This July evening, Eva sits very still as we wait for a breeze to temper the hundred-degree heat. Beyond the patio is "Eva's Compound." A birdhouse with cockatiels, finches, and blue and yellow parrots sits to one side of a narrow wooden walkway. In the gardens beyond, flaming bishop's plume alternates with rows of pink dahlias and crimson gladiolas; zucchini, tomatillos, beans, gourds, and melons fill another plot. The smell of ripe cantaloupe mixes with hay for the beef cattle, llamas, and chickens that live on the acreage in back.

We are about to head for bed when a woman arrives for healing. She is a stranger. But despite the hour and Eva's fatigue, they descend the path to the casita where Eva heals the sick and makes her coronas. Seven-foot sunflowers reach toward a small koi pond in front of the casita. To one side stands a statue of Jesus Christ, whose arms, were they present, would reach out to embrace the world. But vandals shot off the limbs when this statue guarded the

grave of Eva's son Toe (Sergio), who died in a car wreck in 1989.
On the building's front door, an engraved plaque announces,
"Love is all we know on earth and all we need to know." Inside,
shelves brim with jars of dried *yerba buena* and other herbs, massage oil, tiny metal amulets, and icons and statues of Jesus Christ
and the Virgin of Guadalupe.

Eva and her visitor disappear into the casita. I walk back to the
house past tiny Mexican pots strung along the kitchen wall. Jars
of flour, children's toys, and Eva's mother's *metate* and *molcajete*
fill the counter space. Each room is so crammed that Eva's husband, Ted (Teodoro), used to joke that if a fire started, it would
burn for eternity. I wind my way back to the "Guadalupe Room,"
where I sleep. A mountain of pillows is piled on top of the dusty
white lace coverlet on the bed. Books sit on a particleboard shelf:
Travel in Mexico, Richard Bach's *Illusions*, *The Complete Book of
Juicing*, a Catholic missal, and a Bible. A Native American drum
adorns one wall; next to it hangs a certificate of congratulations
from the Pope to Eva's parents on their fiftieth wedding anniver-
sary. Angels engraved, carved, and painted pair up with stuffed
pandas and porcelain dolls. Above the bed, Jesus Christ touches
his sacred heart, but he cannot compete with the Virgin of Guadalupe, whose blue star-studded cloak illuminates an entire wall.
Her benevolent gaze reappears in statues and smaller paintings
throughout the room.

From the bed, I survey the gallery of family photos. "They give
me power," Eva says, "each day when I wake up." I think back to
the hummingbird, pondering the luck that has come to us in the
years since we met. Eva has endured nearly constant assaults—
economic uncertainty, cancer, the death of one son, and the murder of a granddaughter by her own husband's hand—yet I know

Eva would count herself lucky. From the casita comes the sound of her incantation before a *limpia*, a ritual cleansing. Her voice shimmers in the night air.

Two months after my July visit to Nyssa, the Contemporary Crafts Gallery in Portland announces Eva as the recipient of their traditional artist award. I call Eva to see if she will come to town for the ceremony. She breathes deeply before speaking. "Gone, Jo [my nickname], all of it gone. That back room where you always stay, my Guadalupe Room, all my treasures, clothes I made with my hands, my mama's eighty-year-old *rebozos*, my pictures, my parent's fiftieth-anniversary certificate, all my things that give me power when I wake up, Jo, it's all gone. I was pulling weeds when I smelled it. The pump house was on fire. By the time I walked back, my house was burning." She grabbed the phone from the flaming house to call the fire department. "It's a miracle you're alive, lady," said one firemen. "That's what they're saying my whole life," Eva replied.

Two days later, Eva and her daughter Chana (Maria Cristina) drove the nearly four hundred miles to Portland for the Contemporary Crafts awards. My husband, Bob, and I picked them up at a local hotel. Eva emerged in black high heels and a stunning black pantsuit. I knew she'd lost most of her possessions and had no insurance. "Bon marché," she said proudly, fingering the crimson and blue beads that fringed the sleeves.

Eva recalled the fire and its aftermath. "I was scared but I had to get inside to use the phone. I had to call for help. My family was there in a flash. Everyone asking, 'What can I do?'" Little Xochitl (pronounced "so-chee"), Eva's granddaughter born with missing organs and an afflicted heart, arrived with her oxygen tank trailing behind her. "How can I help?" she asked. Eva's voice broke before she resumed. "Now my kids are saying, 'You built the house for us, and now we'll rebuild it for you.' Jo, I'm signing them up. 'If you said you're going to do the French doors, sign right here!'" Eva described one of the only remaining objects from the Guadalupe Room: a piece of pounded copper shaped like a bunch of leaves. "It came out of the fire all shiny. And I thought, 'I will be like that. We will make things shine again.'"

You don't have to share Eva's beliefs to be moved by her life. You don't need to connect faith to religion. Eva's world cannot be reduced to doctrine or dogma, so I try instead to share some of her stories and metaphors. Each chapter begins with an illness, physical or metaphorical—*la enfermedad*—followed by Eva's proposal for healing—*el remedio*. Metaphors, she has taught me, carry us toward what cannot be directly stated. After the fire, Eva described a local woman who cleans houses for a living and came forward to help her. "This," said Eva," is the God I wait for, not some rapturous figure from the clouds. But this woman, short and fat, in denim shorts and bare legs, who comes here after working all day to help me clean my knickknacks damaged by the fire. Here is God."

PART I

The Root

This tree that does not talk taught me the biggest lesson of my life. It was sick and dying; it had no leaves. An old Mexican man told my husband to drill a hole in its trunk, soak a stake with a special recipe, and drive it through that hole. After it [the healing solution] soaked through to the root—less than a month—the tree started to heal. Then the limbs began to produce all these leaves. I learned that when the root is ruined, the limbs are sick, like our heritage that has been stripped and bitten away.

—EVA CASTELLANOZ

I

Measuring Faith

La Enfermedad: If you don't believe, how can you heal?

El Remedio: I choose to believe like a child. I just
believe in the day and whatever it's going to bring me.
I believe in the sun, how beautiful it is. I believe in it
even if it's cloudy and I can't see it. I know it's there.

"FIRST I'M GOING TO SHARE WITH YOU what healing is
to me. Healing starts with yourself. Does anybody know how
much faith weighs? Have you weighed it, anyone?" Eva stands
before an audience of about forty people at the Fishtrap House
in Enterprise, a town in northeast Oregon's Wallowa Mountains.
An elderly rancher in denim overalls, his wife's lap filled with knit-
ting, sits in front; next to them is a ponytailed sculptor drawn here
by the local bronze foundries, snowcapped mountains, and lus-
trous lakes. Writers come to work with Fishtrap, a local literary
organization with a national reach. Few Mexicans live in Enterprise and nearby towns, but many inhabit the edges of Malheur

County, the largest in the state. I've come to hear Eva give a talk about healing practices and Day of the Dead traditions. We drove separately, both arriving late on an October day in 2002. Her ever-problematic car died just as she got to Enterprise. As she speaks, a mechanic at Steve's Shell Station down the road diagnoses the ailment.

Eva's skin glows golden against the stark white of her embroidered blouse. She has told me that she sometimes gets nervous speaking in public, but she never appears anything but supremely confident. She queries the group, "Can you say, 'Yesterday, I had ten pounds of faith. Today I only have one?' Can anybody measure it—I had this much, but now I have this much? Can anybody taste it, like we're tasting food today?" Making eye contact with a young boy in front, Eva continues, "Right now, I don't know what will happen with this car. But I trust. Some people say 'Eva is dumb' because I trust. That's the first thing I ever learned. It has been very, very helpful in my life. Trust. Things happen for a reason."

Eva pins up an embroidered Virgin of Guadalupe cloth as the backdrop to her altar for El Día de los Muertos (The Day of the Dead). In front of the Virgin, she lays out a two-foot skeleton with limp arms and droopy legs. Under its limbs rest tiny black coffins that hint at the losses in Eva's life. A clay whistle sits atop some children's toys. From her woven Mexican bag come pink-iced breads, chocolates, and other treats to honor the dead children—*los angelitos*—whose souls will return on November 1. For the adults who will follow the next day, there are mangoes, apples, oranges, and pomegranates. I've known Eva through a time when she didn't publicly display her altar. She feared being laughed at or harassed by local Anglos when she went to the cemetery. She says,

"I was scared to be who I am, but not anymore." She tells of the first time she summoned the courage to prepare her altar at Nyssa's cemetery. Next to her was a man laying flowers on a grave. He watched Eva silently. "When do you think your dead are coming back to eat those fruits and breads?" he asked. "About the same time your dead return to smell those flowers!" Eva responded. She joins the peals of laughter filling the room, but adds in a serious tone, "I have these lovely customs that were taken away, but I am going to get them back. If your root is sick, the whole of you is going to be sick and I want to heal my root."

Eva's roots reach back to Valle de Santiago, in the Mexican state of Guanajuato. In Mexico, this central fertile region is called the "granary of the republic." Yet, during Eva's childhood, her parents, María Concepción and Fidel Silva, struggled to find food. She describes their lives as she arranges a pile of crimson and gold leaves we had gathered earlier. "Leaves like these were all they had for Day of the Dead. They were too poor to buy offerings." Eva's beliefs and practices creatively mix her parents' heritage with contemporary Mexican American culture in the United States. Her mother descended from the Otomí, an indigenous group who still inhabit the central plateau of Mexico, from the southern city of Toluca to the states of Guanajuato, Hidalgo, and Queretaro.[1] Eva's father called his ancestors la raza de oro, "the golden race" of Aztecs descended from the Nahuatl-speaking peoples who ruled central Mexico at the time of Spanish colonization. "I call myself Mexicana," Eva says. "But truly in my heart, I am Mexica [pronounced 'meh-shee-ca']. The Aztec Indians, that's what they called themselves. That's who I am—an Indian from Mexico."[2]

At the center of her altar in the Fishtrap House, Eva places a small paper hummingbird. In Mexico, the luminous birds are magic. To heal, Eva tells the group, one must understand that nonhuman beings—birds, rocks, a stream—can speak. Some of a *curandera*'s beliefs and practices may seem exotic to an outsider: the soul might spin off from the body, *limpias* cleanse the spirit, and *mal de ojo* (the evil eye) can wreak havoc in a life. But Eva's work is grounded and practical. She blends Western medicine, knowledge of nutrition she learned as an Oregon State University extension agent, and the Mexican and indigenous healing she gleaned from her mother. While each element is important, the gestalt—the source of Eva's healing—is her gift for human connection.

I remember the first time I witnessed her work, on a summer evening a few years after we'd met. We rested on her back patio as a pickup truck screeched up the gravel driveway. A man leaned out to ask for Eva. She rose from her plastic lawn chair to greet him. He exited the truck, his belly hanging above a shiny silver buckle. Three others emerged: a bent elderly woman with gray hair pulled into a bun, a middle-aged woman wrapped in a traditional *rebozo*, and a girl of about eleven. Eva led the way to the casita, where we crowded into the front room. She placed chairs for the family members, indicating that they should remove their shoes. Then she knelt, her long curled hair falling over her shoulders. She drenched her hands with oil from a glass bottle and massaged the feet of each person in turn—the initiation and heart of Eva's healing.

Curanderismo begins with the body but incorporates the spirit and the psyche. Eva now helps colicky children and men with sexual problems. She aids gang members kicked out of school and women bruised by life and lovers and husbands. She welcomes workers from Oregon and Idaho migrant camps and wealthy Anglos from the Boise suburbs. When she treats an individual, she attends to the family and the community. *Curanderismo* is effective, Eva says, because people believe. Faith is the heart of healing and you cannot measure it.

What does it mean to have faith? To believe in anything? To heal from the many fissures in our world? When I witnessed Eva massaging the feet of the members of that family, something in me quickened. Growing up Catholic, I believed that faith was a kind of spontaneous combustion that could ignite the world. Long disenchanted with the institutional church, I still yearn for its rituals. Above all, I long for the fullness of that childhood faith. But when I watch Eva, I am like the men in wide-brimmed hats who arrive from the onion fields. I am like the woman in heels and a tailored suit who drives over from Boise. I am like the family I watched Eva heal on that visit long ago. When we enter her casita, we hear the beating of the hummingbird's wings. We cannot measure faith, but we are swept into its boundless presence.

At that first healing session, Eva presented the man with an amulet to carry as protection against the curse he believed caused his heart palpitations. Then she turned to the women. For them—overworked, underappreciated, and sometimes violated—Eva reserves a cache of healing energy. She gave the older woman aloe vera—a plant Eva calls *siempre viva* (always alive)—for its life-affirming properties. "It will eat up everything negative in the house," Eva promised. She urged the young girl to return for her *quinceañera* preparation when she enters adulthood. She knelt again at feet of the woman with the dark eyes, shrouded under her *rebozo*, looking up to plead, "Save a bit of your grocery money to go to the hairdressers. Buy something for yourself."

Now, Eva picks up this theme for the audience in Enterprise.

"I look to the women," she says, "because I know my people. The women see to the kids first. We're left behind. We're fieldworkers. We're not pretty at night, we're just tired." Eva seems fatigued herself from the long drive and her talk. But she invites the audience forward to examine her altar. Children help her arrange the offerings. She focuses on a skinny boy of twelve or thirteen with chin-length black hair, the only other brown-skinned person in the room. He likely descends from the Nez Perce Indians who live throughout the region. The nearby town of Joseph is named for Chief Joseph, the leader whose flight from the invasion of white settlers ended with his own statement of healing: "I will fight no more." Eva's medical practices may be similar to those used by this boy's ancestors in the era before there was a border to cross, before census data divided Eva as "Hispanic" from him as "Indian." He now adds a child's toy to the altar's sweet breads and spindly skeletons. A blonde woman in flowing robes and turquoise jewelry stands out amid the denim overalls and baseball caps. She fingers the mangoes and asks Eva to come to her house the next day.

Eva turns back to address the larger group. "Life has taught me to believe in miracles, and you're looking at a miracle right now," she says. Eva doesn't tell the audience about the cancer diagnosis more than a decade ago when doctors predicted her imminent demise. She doesn't repeat what she told me the night before: "Death is my sister. This is what I heard growing up. People don't believe it, but I have died, so I know it is true." She doesn't relate that experience of dying that she described the first time I met her and has repeated many times since. She doesn't relate any of the traumas that make her appearance at the Fishtrap House this day highly unlikely. She just tells this story:

There was a very rich person who had all this land and so many
beautiful things. One day, a man, called the master, walked
onto the rich man's land without knowing it. To the master,
there were no boundaries. He had with him a child who had
come to learn the master's ways. The owner of the place met
up with them and demanded, "What are you doing here? This
is my land." The master told him who he was and the rich man
said, "Oh, I have heard of you and your miracles. I have been
walking and I am very thirsty. Make water for me! I want to
see these miracles." So the master said, "Did you see the sunrise this morning?" The rich man got angry, "What does that
have to do with anything? I want to see miracles." But the master didn't make any miracles. The rich man got tired and left.
The master and the child continued to walk. The child found a
rabbit lying on the ground, nearly dead. The master picked him
up and blew on him and he hopped away. He found a sick bird,
kissed him, and the bird flew. They were thirsty and stopped by
a tree. The master tapped the trunk of the tree and water came.
The child was so surprised, "Why didn't you do that when the
rich man asked you to?" The master said, "What is the use? He
doesn't see the miracle in the sunrise."

"I learned this story from my parents," Eva said. "People sometimes call it New Age. My parents didn't know about such things.
They didn't even read. I have my daddy's Bible. He learned to read
a little later in his life. I open up his Bible sometimes when I need
him and I see the scribbles of a three-year-old. But the stories still
gave him assurance. They give me assurance. New Age? I think
this is very old age."

The woman with the turquoise jewelry smiles. Everyone
approaches to shake Eva's hand and welcome her. We will return
tomorrow for her workshop on traditional Mexican arts. I help
Eva rearrange the offerings and cover the altar. With a final glance

at the Virgin, we leave for Steve's Shell station. Stars thicken a cobalt sky. The late October air feels brisk against our skin. The mechanic, like everyone in this rural town, is irrepressibly friendly. His craggy face lights up as we approach, "Well, it's your lucky day! It was the fuel pump. She's ready to roll now." When Eva reaches for her wallet, the mechanic places a hand on her arm. "You know, I said it was your lucky day." He shakes his head and grins. "Somebody came by and paid for it earlier."

2

The Story Too Big to Tell

La Enfermedad: Later in my life, I knew [about her
parents' suffering]. Things happened to me like
that; you lose your mind. You don't remember.

El Remedio: My parents could remember. When
I think of the stories they used to tell us, it's like
a fairy tale. It's not real, but to us, it's real.

IN 1942, MARÍA CONCEPCIÓN JUÁREZ SILVA, known as
"Conchita" to her family, left Valle de Santiago, Mexico, with her
husband, José Loreto Fidel Silva. Their hands must have tightly
clasped those of three-year-old Eva. Born Genoveva Silva Juárez
on November 18, 1939, Eva was the only child out of six who was
still alive. Conchita carried a few things for the trip north to the
border: her small statues of El Santo Niño de Atocha and La Virgen de San Juan, her *molcajete* to macerate chilies into salsa, and
her *metate* for grinding corn. These objects, perhaps, would temper the hardships of starting a new life in Texas. Conchita didn't

yet know that she would have to leave her precious possessions at the ranch near Reynosa, where they would await the coyote who would bring them across the border.

Perhaps Eva's parents were tempted to abandon their stories there, too. Pieces of their Mexican past may have felt too heavy to carry. But they couldn't help themselves. They crossed with their stories, and they passed them on to Eva.

Valle de Santiago lies in the central Bajío region of the Mexican state of Guanajuato. When Eva's family lived in town, families would gather on Sunday afternoons in the central *jardín* and La Plaza de la Independencia. A few blocks away stood the church of Valle's patron saint, Santiago. On his feast day, the town closed down to celebrate. As a child, Fidel Silva would watch as horsemen flew past the church, catching live roosters strung upside down along clotheslines stretched high above the streets. Beyond, rising in ever smaller layers like the top of a wedding cake, was the red and white steeple of the Church of La Merced, Our Lady of Mercy; Eva's mother sewed doilies for the altar and vestments for the priest. Nine other Catholic churches built during the Spanish colonization between the fifteenth and the eighteenth centuries punctuated the landscape.

The small town that Eva's parents inhabited rested on what had been the indigenous village of Camémbaro—a Purépecha word for the healing herbs *estafiate* or *ajenjo* (Artemisia) that grow in the region. Today, productive fields of broccoli, cauliflower, and onions surround a bustling urban center with a population of 130,000. Still, traditional celebrations and stories persevere. Many tell about the thermal sulphuric lakes that fill the ruins of extinguished volcanoes. Local people called them Las Siete Luminarias (the seven lights or illuminations). The big dipper hovers overhead and mimics the shape of the volcanic lakes, linking heavenly and earthly patterns.[1] In one of those lakes, La Alberca, people used to bathe; they believed the lake's waters held magical powers. Eva's father told her that La Alberca mysteriously arose one day from a tiny *ojo de agua*—an "eye of water" or geyser. In ancient times, he said, the lake roared day and night. The waters quieted only after La Alberca was christened and then got married to Paricutín, a volcano in Michoacán.

If not for La Alberca, Eva's parents might never have crossed paths. Conchita grew up on a prosperous hacienda. When her father, Francisco Juárez, died, her mother, Soledad Marez, continued to oversee the workers. Soledad was a powerful woman, who rode through the fields wearing a huge black cape of corn husks. Conchita learned embroidery and crafts and kept her hands soft and unmarked by manual labor. When Soledad died suddenly, Conchita moved to her grandmother's house. "Her brothers didn't want anything to do with her because she was a little girl," Eva says. "At her grandmother's, she had to scrub floors and wash dishes."

Fidel Silva, too, was essentially orphaned. After his mother, Juana Ruíz, died, his grandmother, who passed on her Silva name, raised him for a time. But his father, José Guadalupe Zavala, decided to send him to a Catholic orphanage. "He couldn't stand it there," Eva recalls. "He ran away to Mexico City. He was probably about ten. Nobody took care of him, so he lived on the streets with older people who taught him to drink. He was hungry a lot and when he was hungry, he drank."

From Conchita's grandmother's home, you could toss a stone into La Alberca. One day, Fidel ascended the hill to bathe. Conchita was on her front porch bent over her embroidery. "She was with her grandma, doing handiwork, like a lot of Mexican women do," Eva says. "My mommy was only fourteen years old. My dad saw her and he wanted her, so he took her. Just like an object."

Fidel Silva had already been married. His first wife died in childbirth, leaving him with two boys, Margarito and Guadalupe. "He needed someone to take care of them," Eva says of her father's motives for marriage. "For many years, I asked him, 'Why did you marry my mom?' I wanted in my soul for him to tell me that he loved her. But all he said was 'I needed a woman to take care of my children and make me tortillas.' She didn't know him and maybe that's why she didn't love him. He stole her. That's how things were done then. You like somebody, you take her. If you're a señorita, and someone takes you, you have to stay with him because if you don't, you're disgraced forever. So she stayed."[2]

Eva's parents grew up in the first decades of the twentieth century, a time of economic and political upheaval in Mexico. The state of Guanajuato had thrived in the eighteenth and nineteenth centuries as a source of silver for Europe. But in 1907, a worldwide financial crisis shattered Mexico's mining industry. A drought followed in 1908–09, ruining half of the country's wheat harvest and leaving the northern states particularly impoverished. The tumult of the Mexican Revolution filled the decade from 1910 to 1920. Fidel Silva later told Eva how the *revolucionarios* stole their corn; his mother gleaned the remaining kernels to grind for tortillas. During the revolution, many fought the long rule of Porfirio Díaz. His thirty-four-year leadership under the motto "Order and Progress" centralized economic and political structures, but it did so at the expense of traditional local autonomy.[3] Village groups fought Porfirian "progress." Many sought social and economic justice for

put him on the burro. So, they waited until he got better. There are a lot of very, very sad stories."

Eva's parents' tale might have taken a different turn. They might have overcome the hardships of their stormy marriage if economic opportunities had opened up. Perhaps they would have sold their handmade furniture in the market, as both were creative *artesanos*. Fidel carved the wooden chairs for which Conchita wove caned seats from tules. She painted bright flowers and hummingbirds on the wooden backs. They could have gleaned nourishment from the fields or even owned some land. In the 1930s, the Lazaro Cárdenas land reforms redistributed plots to peasants and villagers. But if such political movements touched Eva's parents, those stories never filtered down to Eva.

I've gone to Valle de Santiago twice. Once, I stood at the edge of the now dry La Alberca and imagined the legends about Las Siete Luminarias. Later, at the downtown museum, the docent confirmed that locals still tell those tales. I've taped, transcribed, and reread Eva's stories many times; still, as scribe to her *testimonios*, I struggle to understand. How do we comprehend narratives so different from those that shape our own experience? Eva has told me, "When I think of the stories my parents used to tell us, it's like a fairy tale. It's not real, but to us, it's real." When I've asked her to elaborate, Eva has said, "People don't believe the things that happen to me. To others, it's like a fairy tale, like Goldilocks."

These bare bones of stories echo fairy tales in their recurrent motifs—the orphaned boy running away, the little girl left to scrub floors, the family on the edge of survival in the woods. They recall the darkness of *märchen*, European folktales that nineteenth-century collectors sanitized before publication. Trained as a folklorist, I'm tempted to analyze Eva's stories about her parents. Do they cleanse her psyche of trauma, as some believe fairy tales do? I want to know when the transformation will come, as it does in such tales. But the rush to explain, I remember, can destroy enchantment. Stories are a magical world where anything can happen; unseen forces rule.[4] Eva calls the experience of stories "God talking" to her; others may call it, as the tellers of old tales did, "wonder." Wonder reminds me that I cannot truly imagine living in the woods with six children—a life of dislocation and poverty. Yet, through narrative, I can briefly inhabit some of its dimensions—despair as well as survival. This is where I am from, Eva's stories tell me, a place where people suffered. This is who I am—a person who hopes.

Still, one story that Eva relates challenges my imagination:

The five children my parents had before me were Víctor, Manuel, Trinidad, Tomás, and Teresa. That was a very hard time for them; they did not have a home. When their children got sick, people were afraid to help them. They thought, "Their kids are sick; we're going to get sick, too." They were so poor— my mommy would show with her hands open that they didn't have the twenty-cent piece that would bring their healing. All she knew [about healing] was exhausted. I don't really know what came over those children that they got so ill all together. They all died, all within a month. She could remember. My parents could remember and they told us. They walked the streets, looking for somewhere they could stay in a corner with their children. I can't remember right now if my mom said, "We had two live ones and three dead" or if it was "three live ones and two dead." I think one of them she stuffed in a pot, so it must have been big enough that she could stuff one of her children in there. They put the other ones in a box. I don't know how they were carrying the two or three live ones that they still had. They all died anyway.

They had to bury their children, like clandestine. They didn't have the money to pay the law to do it. They didn't even know where they could take a flower to the grave. They forgot, they just did it.

Later in my life, I knew. Things happened to me like that; you lose your mind. You don't remember. So that's the story of these two parents that lost five children within a month.

Eva told this story when we met, and I carry it with me—a *testimonio* of affliction. Telling stories can both resuscitate and relieve pain. They are, as Canadian writer Ted Chamberlain has said, "a walk in the storm and a shelter from it."[5] Eva's stories remind me that the cure for unbearable loss is the same as the illness: remembering.

Eva's parents never returned to Valle de Santiago. Eva has gone twice—once briefly with her husband, Ted, once with her sister, Gorda (María Teresa, whose nickname means "fat"). Both trips triggered dark memories of her parents' stories. "It was so hard, Jo. I could not bear to be there. My relatives came, and it is our custom to bring offerings of food. But I couldn't be happy. The women were getting the big pots together to make chocolate with bread, but I couldn't bear it; my heart was heavy. They kept putting light to my face, saying, 'Come, come and see her! She looks exactly like Fidel! Nothing like Conchita!' I wanted to—I still want to—have heart enough to go and walk where my mom walked in tears from the life she was living, where my dad had to struggle to feed us where the children died. It's almost like it's just so big that it still lingers in your thoughts, just by saying it and not even living it."

Just by saying it. You lose your mind; you don't remember. It's like a fairy tale. It's not real, but to us, it's real. Eva carries with her the tale of monumental loss from which there seems to be no healing, the story that cannot be understood yet must be told.

Eva's parents made that first crossing into the United States without the *metate, molcajete,* and *santos* that Conchita had carried north. They settled in Texas with Eva. Two sons, Manuel and Diego, followed the birth of Gorda, their younger daughter. Some years passed before Conchita could cross the Rio Grande again to retrieve her possessions from the ranch where she'd left them. Her Santo Niño de Atocha now rests on Eva's altar, the *metate* and *molcajete* live in her kitchen in Nyssa. "She gave me power through that stone," Eva says of the *metate* passed down from mother to daughter, and years later rescued from the fire that destroyed Eva's house, repeatedly reclaimed. The old French, *reclamer,* means "to call back, appeal to." The Spanish *reclamar* suggests calling attention to something that is not quite right. In Latin, *reclamare* signifies to "cry out against." Thus, Eva reclaims stories of her parents' life in Valle de Santiago with each telling.

3

Crossing Over

La Enfermedad: We'd cross the Rio Grande,
like going out on a very thin branch. People
would say, "Don't take your little girl! She
could get raped; you could get raped."

El Remedio: My mama had to do it to feed her
babies. She was brave. We risked our lives; she
risked my life. Now, this would be called child
abuse. But you know what? She taught me courage.
She was preparing me for my whole life.

AT FALFURRIAS, TEXAS—the U.S. Border Patrol checkpoint
with the highest seizure rate in the country—a beefy, uniformed
guard steps up to our car. Silver-rimmed sunglasses slip down his
nose as he leans into the window. A German shepherd hovers at
his heels. "Identification?" he asks. When I reach for my license, I
glimpse Eva's trembling hands. She holds up proof of the permanent resident status she's held since she was a teenager. "Were you

scared as a child, living without legal papers?" I ask as we drive away. Eva's eyes widen. "It didn't end then, Jo," she says. "I am still afraid."

Eva and I are driving south on Highway 281 to Pharr, the town where she spent her childhood and adolescence. I've heard Texas stories for over a decade. Now Eva wants to show me the markers of her past, sites of hardship and pleasure. We had hoped to stop near Falfurrias at the shrine of folk saint "Don Pedrito." Don Pedro Jaramillo was a nineteenth-century *curandero*. His legendary healing powers continue to draw pilgrims from throughout the United States and Mexico. Eva's stories of the shrine deepened my interest in his legacy and the power of faith among people in the borderlands. But our Falfurrias checkpoint experience has discouraged further exploration. We head for Pharr, where we will stay with Eva's daughter, Chayo (Rosario) and her family, long-time residents.

White pillars and arcs decorated with wrought-iron horses or bulls announce ranchos along the road. At the highway's edge, mistletoe hangs from spindly trees. Mesquite and prickly pear, sage and oak add subtle color to the dry land. Occasional clouds form scallop shells overhead, breaking the heat as we drive. Approaching Edinburg, we rise over a hill onto Freddy Gonzales Drive. All at once, we're in the Rio Grande Valley.

Eva and I met the night before at the San Antonio airport. It's October 2001, eerily quiet a month after the 9/11 attacks. Eva's discomfort at Falfurrias surprises me; I think of her as fearless. But post-9/11, pervasive fear deepens the long-standing border tensions.

Crossing a border can shake even a firm identity, but we are now entering an unofficial country where identities are already blurred:

Mexican South Texas, the wellspring of "Greater Mexico"—Mexican culture wherever it is lived.[1] Locals eat *barbacoa* (meat slow-cooked over an open fire or underground), play *lotería* (a Mexican game similar to Bingo), and listen to *conjunto* music (also called *norteño* and distinguished by the use of the accordion and *bajo sexto*, a twelve-stringed instrument).They attend *peleas de gallo* (cockfights) and *charreadas* (rodeo); they also shop at Costco and Kmart. Most speak English as fluently as Spanish. That Mexicans (and Native Americans) were here long before Anglos arrived is an established fact. The Mexican eagle and serpent hang alongside the Stars and Stripes in the Brownsville statehouse. Yet, vigilante groups, now buoyed by 9/11 fear, stand poised to slam the border shut as though it could be made as impenetrable as the wall some hope to erect. In fact, for two centuries, the border has opened and closed like a river's locks whenever it suited the U.S. government. Because we need the workers who cross each day, the border is a useful myth, writes William Langewiesche. "It acts as a filter crossed by the energetic and the brave."[2]

Memories of other crossings reverberate for Eva as we drive under the domed sky toward Pharr. When her parents arrived in 1942, her mother carried a vision of El Otro Lado (the Other Side). "She got all dressed up to cross. She'd bought a new dress—white with blue bells—sandals, and stockings. She never used to wear such things, but she bought them because she thought nobody was ugly over here, that it was paved, that there were no weeds." The family waited at a ranch outside Reynosa for the coyote. "We called them *pateros* then," Eva explains the reference from *pato*, Spanish for "duck," establishing a connection to "wetbacks." The night was dark, the river low. The *patero* took Eva and her parents to the river, where a canoe with about eighteen people awaited them. Crossing over, excess weight toppled the boat. Everybody panicked. She recalls now, "My mom said it was really scary, really dark. We found each other but my mom had to slide down the riverbank through mud and weeds. There goes her dress and hose. She thought everything here would be easy, that money was just easy to get. She found out it wasn't like that."

Today, Conchita would be forgiven for thinking money is "just easy to get." Signs offer quick credit for new cars and RVs along the highway into town. We're five miles west of McAllen in booming south-central Hidalgo County. Billboards welcome the "winter Texans" whose seasonal dollars fuel this city of forty-six thousand residents, 90 percent of whom are Latino. Thick traffic crawls past strip malls and scores of Denny's restaurants, Days Inns, and Best Westerns. Huge fruit warehouses overflow with locally grown watermelons, oranges, and grapefruit. Downtown, Esperanza's unisex hair salon stands across from the now defunct Texas Hotel and a chow mein parlor. The Healing Hands Center offers massage and acupuncture along with Mexican *curanderismo*. We stop for gas and pick up the chamber of commerce brochures touting the area's attractions: the two-thousand-acre Santa Ana National Wildlife Refuge four miles east of town, Smitty's Juke Box Museum, Ye Old Clock Museum, and Moreno's Feed Store–Pet Stores and Zoo, with its three- and four-legged chickens and exotic snakes.

The official brochures trace Pharr's beginnings to 1909, when Henry N. Pharr, a sugarcane plantation owner from Louisiana, and John C. Kelly of Waco, Texas, bought twenty thousand acres for $17.50 an acre. They founded the Louisiana and Rio Grande Canal Company and constructed an irrigation system to grow sugarcane. Seven years later, the city incorporated. The brochures do not go back to the Spanish government's land grant in 1767 to Juan José Hinojosa. Though his family sold off parcels to various groups in the late nineteenth century, they remained a presence in the area until the 1880s.[3] Mention of the long residence and contributions of Mexicans and Mexican Americans is curiously absent.

Earlier, we mistakenly detoured off the straight highway from San Antonio and landed in Corpus Christi. Eva and I share a talent for, as she says, "getting lost in a glass of water." We are now very late for dinner at Chayo's, but I still slow down whenever Eva spots a place she recognizes. We drive by *la primera frontera*—an empty culvert and the first border before the river. The true border, the Pharr-Reynosa International Bridge, is closed because of the 9/11 attacks. Eva scans a field for signs of the shack where her family once lived. After that first crossing, they worked the fields and established a life in Pharr. When immigration authorities found them, they sent the family back to Reynosa to await processing of their application for residency. Eva's father, she says, feared *la migra* (the Immigration and Naturalization Service); he stayed on the Mexican side until their papers cleared. But her mother was lost without her connections for selling chickens and making money in Pharr; no such network existed for her yet in Reynosa. So Conchita crossed back and forth each day, taking Eva with her.

"My mother had to do it," says Eva. "She had to cross to get milk for her babies after my sister, Gorda, then my brothers, Fidel and Manuel, were born. We'd cross the Rio Grande, like going onto a very thin branch! People would say, 'Don't take your little girl there because she could get raped, you could get raped.' But we had to get milk for the babies. So we walked across the river. She knew where by the color of the water. She was brave."

Beyond the river lay another hurdle—a large cattle ranch

owned by a German family. "At El Rancho de los Alemanes, they had longhorn cattle with sharp pointy horns, and you know I was scared! But my mom was not afraid. She would take handfuls of dirt and throw them at the cattle. Even if the dirt was just a symbol, the longhorns wouldn't even look up. Her symbols, her faith, her daring, her love for her babies made her do that. She dragged me with her and I learned." As we drive on, Eva remembers, "We risked our lives. She risked my life. Now, this would be called child abuse. But you know what? She taught me courage. She was preparing me for my whole life."

Where Eva's first house after marriage once stood is now a row of shops; a strip of car dealerships on the highway to Reynosa shelters ghosts of a once thriving neighborhood. Little remains of Eva's childhood world except her stories.

A shrine to the Virgin encased in blue and white tiles illuminates Chayo and Ricardo Garcia's front yard. Chayo, Eva's second child and eldest daughter, greets us warmly. Her soft-featured beauty and statuesque figure create a presence as commanding as that of her husband, who towers over all of us at more than six feet tall. Chayo met Ricardo at a migrant camp in Idaho; they later moved back to Pharr. Two of their three children—Chata (Rosa Elia) and Juna (Rosario) have moved out on their own. Only J. R. (Ricardo Jr.) still lives at home, waiting to marry his Mexican girlfriend. He is handsome and attentive, leaping up when Chayo asks for something. J. R. works for a manufacturer in nearby Edinburg that produces items like the cup holder he immediately gives me. The front reads "Proud to be an American/United We Stand." Though we're hours late, the family has waited to eat. We sit down to tuna patties, pinto beans, Mexican rice, homemade spicy salsa, and tortillas. Chata arrives while we're eating, with children in tow—the three Eva calls "the termites" and little Jenny (Genoveva), named for Eva. They laugh and joke as we devour the meal after our long trip; the family puts me immediately at ease.

After dinner, Eva camps on the couch under a Mickey Mouse quilt. The bedroom is reserved for me as the guest. At around four in the morning, the bathroom door squeaks open, then again at five and six as Ricardo, Chayo, and J.R. prepare for long days at work. The family's work ethic, shared by all her children, fills Eva with pride. The next morning, we begin our search for the places where her parents, the source of that ethic, once worked. Fidel Silva served as foreman at the Browns' farm. He worked directly for Mr. Brown, escaping the brokers who assembled and often exploited work crews. "He wanted a better life," Eva says. "Especially after their children died in Mexico."

Between 1910 and 1930, almost one-eighth of Mexico's population shifted north, driven by civil war and economic instability. In the United States, mines, railroads, and especially farms needed workers. During World War I, the secretary of labor waived all immigration restrictions for Mexicans. The 1921 Immigration Act tightening European immigration again exempted Mexicans, listing them as "white" to bypass race quotas. But the economic failures of the Great Depression eclipsed their temporary welcome. In the 1930s, the U.S. government repatriated about one-third of immigrants from Mexico, including the 60 percent who were citizens born in the United States.[4] Throughout that time, Fidel Silva crossed the Rio Grande again and again to feed his family.

With the outbreak of World War II, renewed demands for cheap labor reopened the border. In 1942, the two governments formalized the crossing of Mexican laborers with the Emergency Labor

Program; approval of Public Law 45, known as the Bracero Program, followed. In the next five years, 219,000 workers arrived in the United States from Mexico. Braceros bolstered the American economy; they also faced multiple hardships. Public Law 45 stipulated that braceros receive minimum wage, health care, adequate housing and board, and protection against discrimination. In fact, many men lived in tents with little protection from summer heat and winter chill; the lack of iron-rich food caused anemia. They faced the constant threat of accidents and the brunt of ongoing racial discrimination.[5] Fidel Silva once broke a leg falling from a truck full of contracted workers in Nyssa. For years, he worked with a leg brace.

Eva, like many children, labored in the fields with her family. About their years on the Browns' farm, Eva says, "My daddy taught me to work, and I am not scared to do anything. He didn't expect anything less of me than of the men, even though I was seven years old and skinnier than a twig. There would be a grown-up man to my right, another one to my left. I was in the middle, trudging through the mud with a gunnysack for cabbage or tomatoes or whatever they were planting. As soon as I got to the other end, I had to turn around and start again. Those men could not catch up with me! I cannot remember being tired. But I also cannot remember being a child. I was a little girl-woman."

Eva's experience echoes that of many children catapulted into the adult work world. Migrant workers had few avenues for fighting discrimination, child labor, and other issues. Excluded from the 1935 National Labor Relations Act, they could not organize; when they tried, they met violent resistance. In the 1960s, César Chávez broke through that barrier to rally migrant laborers in California. In 1966, workers in the Rio Grande Valley attempted to organize in a similar fashion. The attempt was, in Rodolfo Acuña's words, "brief, fiery, and tumultuous."[6] After a series of thwarted strikes and demonstrations, Chávez pulled back to focus on California and, eventually, on federal legislation to protect workers. Despite their numbers, Latinos in the Rio Grande Valley had little power or public presence until the 1970s. The year of the "Pharr Riot," 1971, marked a turning point in the Chicano rights movement in the valley. A peaceful protest against police brutality erupted into violence, but it also pushed social change.[7] Around the same time, Texas clothing workers organized strikes at Levi Strauss and other major companies, breaking the deadlock. In 1975, the Texas Farm Workers organized; two years later, they gathered at the Lincoln Memorial in Washington DC to demand rights for undocumented workers.[8] But by that time, Eva and her family had been in Oregon for nearly two decades.

As Eva recaptures her memories, I can almost smell the orange groves surrounding the Browns' farm. Almost, for the landscape she remembers is gone. She seems pensive as we circle back to the house. When Chayo returns from her job as a Head Start teaching assistant, we depart for a tour of Pharr. But we don't see Ye Old Clock Museum or Smitty's Jukeboxes or Moreno's three-legged chickens. We see schools—the paths to upward mobility in America. We pass the Lyndon B. Johnson Middle School, but also elementary schools named for Garcías and Ramírezes. The south side of Pharr showcases shiny structures with modern sports facilities and computer labs. Chayo is passionate about her work and wants to move from assistant to teacher. But with days full of work and family, the dream of more education seems remote. Still, Chayo displays the flash of determination that illuminates her mother. I imagine the day when she will inhabit her own classroom.

We turn onto Flag Street to find Napper Elementary, the school Eva attended. As a child, she fought formal schooling; going to the fields with her father each day formed her education. But Methodist missionaries began visiting the farm. "They wanted to convert us to their religion. They said it was time for school, I guess, or so they thought. We cried, my daddy and I, because we had been together for so long, and now it was time for me to go and learn English, which he called the 'language of the angels.'"

At the end of her first day of school, other students boarded buses for home. Eva stood alone, unable to ask the English-speaking teachers for help. She remembered what her father taught her about fear. "He would say, 'Who did you rob? Who did you kill?' Then, you cannot fear.'" What she did fear was missing out on the meat they had found at the dump that morning. Her father would skin the animal—in this case, a cow—then dry it with spices to a jerky-like consistency. Eva sat with her head down outside the school, fretting about losing her share. The one student who remained took her by the hand onto the last bus. At the girl's house, where no one spoke Spanish, Eva cried all night. The next day, the police came. "Heck if I was ever going back to school," Eva says. "For the longest time, I didn't even want to hear that word."

But Eva grew to love school, hopscotching across grades, sometimes promoted twice in one year. "Teachers didn't know what to do with me because I was a super-smart little girl. I could go places in books—that's why I liked it so much. It was a way out." Her escape into books and writing reaped rewards, including placing third in a poetry contest. Eva couldn't wait to go to the finals to read her poem, but her mother forebade it. "She didn't want us reading even funny books. She couldn't read English, so if she didn't know what it was, we couldn't read it." Eva also loved sports. "At school, I could play baseball. Everybody wanted me on their team. I was good! I could do a lot of things I couldn't do at home."

Eva's school had a mix of Anglo and Mexican students. Until 1925, Mexicans had attended a separate elementary school. No secondary facilities existed for them because the government assumed they wouldn't go beyond the elementary level. Even after a high school was built, some housing and education facilities remained segregated until the 1970s.

At dinnertime, Chata arrives with "the termites," decked out in Superman and monster costumes. We drive to a Kelly Street food stand owned by Ricardo's brother. Sitting at picnic tables in the balmy autumn air, we eat grilled corn on wooden skewers. The owner plies passers-by with promotional flyers stapled to bags of candy corn. Halloween accoutrements are far more visible here than El Día de los Muertos altars. Eva laments the long-standing dominance of the American holiday here as well as in eastern Oregon. "People just aren't doing it," she says of Mexican traditions. "At home, I have to leave Nyssa and go to Portland to see people putting up their Los Muertos altars." We witness a similar absence of Mexican practices the next morning when Eva and I visit Dead Man's Cemetery. Families dig up weeds and adorn graves with flowers. But we see none of the sugar skulls, tiny caskets, or other altar offerings that fill Mexican graveyards.

This pattern appears to be shifting. Each year, cities in both the United States and Mexico are witnessing a more visible blending of traditions. In Mexico City, kids now roam the streets with masks and jack-o'-lanterns, begging treats or money. "Halloween" is sometimes spelled *jaloguin*, reports the *Los Angeles Times*, as in the statement, "The Roman Catholic Church requests that the faithful refrain from celebrating that pagan American holiday known as *jaloguin*."[9] Just as Halloween infiltrates Mexico, Day of the Dead gains ground in the United States. The celebration has grown nearly as child-centered as Halloween—a key difference from the community-wide feeling in Mexico. Children's books such as George Acona's *Pablo Remembers: The Fiesta of the Day of the Dead* form part of multicultural curricula in many schools.[10] Museums, including Portland's Oregon History Center, regularly invite Latino artists such as Eva to create traditional altars. Schools stress the holiday's secular aspects and the universal dimension of rites of passage surrounding death. But in Mexican South Texas, the thick braid of cultures, of secular and sacred, is hard to tease apart.

Eva bows her head in thought as we leave the cemetery. I wonder what she had hoped to discover in this place that triggers memories of childhood joy as well as fear. We'd driven south in search of the world Eva's parents risked their lives to create for her and her siblings. Eva has returned as a pilgrim, not just a visitor. The distinction, Cynthia Ozick writes, is that "a visitor passes through a place, the place passes through a pilgrim."[11] Ozick's phrase echoes a Mexican *dicho*, a popular saying: *No cruzé la frontera, la frontera me cruzó a mi* (I didn't cross the border, the border crossed through me). Perhaps Eva craves all of it again: the passage, the fear, and the courage, the sundering from which she emerged whole. Perhaps she wanted me to witness that crossing through reenactment. But the Pharr-Reynosa International Bridge remains closed. Eva decides to stay for a week. She wants to search for an old friend she hasn't tracked down, for something in her past yet to be uncovered. I plan my departure for San Antonio.

On our last day, we journey to nearby San Juan. The shiny metal cross of the Basilica of Our Lady of San Juan del Valle rises in the distance. Black and white mosaics above the entrance greet the ten thousand visitors who journey here every weekend. To one side stands the original church. It was built in 1954 in honor of a Mexican shrine in Jalisco to La Virgen de San Juan de los Lagos. We can't go inside the old church, but I imagine it is sizeable. In 1966, a thousand striking workers organized by the United Farm Workers Organizing Committee attended mass here. Four years later, a crazed pilot drove through the steeple, nearly destroying the building. The story seems both more and less bizarre than it would have before 9/11.

We enter the new basilica through massive bronze doors decorated with symbols of faith, hope, and charity. Eva and I slip past the main chapel, where the priest's Spanish lilts over a hundred or so pilgrims. An adjacent room brims with abandoned crutches, billowy white bridal gowns, used *coronas* from *quinceañeras*, and sky-blue graduation dresses. Photos adorn a wall above a box for *ofrendas* (offerings). On sheets of black velvet hang tiny gold legs and arms—*milagros* that testify to miracles prayed for and perhaps granted. Eva and I kneel before the crutches. I watch her lips move and wonder for whom she prays. She might conjure the spirits of her dead siblings or her son Toe; perhaps she envisions her granddaughter Xochitl, the oxygen tank trailing behind her. She might think of her daughter Chana and her husband forced out of their jobs in California by a racist store manager. Her Texas family must figure in her prayers—Chayo's struggle to become a teacher and Chata's hardships as a single mother to "the termites." Perhaps Eva prays that the courage that fueled her mother's crossing stays alive in each descending generation. Outside the *milagro*

room, we fill small plastic bottles with holy water from stone cis-
terns. Mine will be confiscated when I pass through airport security the next day.

————————

Home in Portland, I reread *After Silence*, a memoir I use to teach
writing and gender studies. In her story of recovering from a bru-
tal rape, Nancy Venable Raine details how violence shatters the
spirit as profoundly as the body and psyche. She writes that "the
opposite of fear is not, I think, courage. It is faith."[12] As I read,
memories of my trip to Pharr return. Two images compete: Eva's
hands at the Falfurrias checkpoint, and Eva kneeling in the milagro room. Then the impressions merge. For Eva, faith is the opposite of fear. Faith is neither conservative nor static. Faith is a form
of continual movement, like Conchita Silva crossing the river to
get milk for her babies. Faith is the symbolic toss of the dirt to
keep away the longhorn cattle. Faith is the walk out on "a very
slim branch," finding your way in a world that doesn't speak your
language or share your symbols. As I read, my fingers caress the
edges of the book, feeling its borders.

4

La Mula

La Enfermedad: I suffered so much because I
didn't fit in. I was different, wore long braids,
and sold chickens with my mother. People
put me in a box and made fun of me.

El Remedio: I don't want to be like everybody else.
If something is true or right to me, I will do it no
matter if I'm alone on that path. I'm *la mula* of
my family. I am very willful and I will myself.

HOW DID IT EMERGE, the spirit of *la mula* (the mule), the stubborn one who sees differently?

Perhaps it began in utero, for Eva believes she absorbed
lessons before she was born. "I knew about healing from the
time I was in the womb," she says. Perhaps she also glimpsed
the path she would follow. Imagine *la mula*'s spirit clinging
to her mother, reluctant to be born with the *don*, or gift. For
it is said that the child who cries in the womb resists birth,

knowing she will come to bear the heavy responsibilities of being a healer.[1]

Eva knew early on that she was different—an *india* (Indian woman). In the 1940s, "upward mobility could not include an Indian presence."[2] She came of age in an era when indigenous identity brought even greater shame than being Mexican American. "I would be embarrassed when my daddy talked to the plants," Eva says of her time in the fields of the Rio Grande Valley with her father. "It seems like a dream now, but we would leave the house with two little *gorditas* [thick tortillas] my mother packed. Along the way, he would pray to the plants, trading pieces of the *gorditas*. When we were hungry, he would find a place with water. I didn't see anything, but there were fish in there. He would run his hat under the water, then wrap the fish in his piece of *gordita*. He'd make himself a fire and then feed me. The earth, the rocks—I think those were his only friends."

Eva's mother maintained other indigenous traditions. "Each night, she would get tomatoes to put on our hair," Eva remembers. "Then she would braid it and wrap it with banana leaves, no matter how tired she was." Conchita Silva worked in the fields all day and then cooked for thirty-five men. "She worked plus! They were branding animals and had to castrate the calves. She picked tomatoes, cotton, then rushed home to make lunch and dinner." Eva describes the time-consuming food rituals: "She ground the corn on her *molcajete*, then put the *masa* on the *metate*, spread it with her hand, put chili on it. Then *la carne* [the meat]: she would roll it into cakes, then put on the husk, cover, and boil it." Her mother made soap from the "bile of a *toro*—it had to be a bull." Conchita also practiced Otomí healing, performing *limpias* (cleansing rituals) for workers and prescribing herbs for illness.

Eva eventually turned her difference from a source of shame to pride. "I learned to love it," she says of her parents' practices. She listened to the songs her parents created and sang to one another and to the rocks and streams. "The things that don't talk teach me so much," Eva says of the plants, stones, and animals whose language she understands. "My daddy said it was a miracle, life. About the water in the canal, '*Ella te habla*' (She will talk to you), he said. He taught me to listen to the trees, the sounds of the water as it goes over different rocks. What are they saying?"

When Fidel Silva pressed the dew onto his daughter's eyes to show her that she would "see differently," he might have unknowingly nurtured her resistance. One day, her father told Eva not to cross the fields of squash. "Why not?" she asked. Because she was a girl, he said, the plants would die. "He said it in an innocent way." Eva describes his traditional beliefs about women as polluting. "But even in an innocent way, it wasn't good. You see, he did it to *la mula*, the one who was not going to take it into her soul." Eva had to find out for herself. That night, she walked across the fields. "If the *calabazas* had been dead the next morning, I wouldn't have done it anymore. But I found out it's not true. That's one of our beliefs that has to die! And if it doesn't die for others, it is dead for me. Later, he said, 'Oh, well when you're in your *sangre*, you know, when you bleed.' Well, I waited [for menstruation]. Then, I told him, 'Tata, they didn't die. You lied! And you said it's not good to lie.' Then, he would just look at me, '*Ay! Eres una mula* [You are a mule]!'"

Perhaps Eva foresaw that resistance within the family would one day extend to a larger world.

"The first time I remember being *la mula* I was just small, maybe six. I saw a lot of things that weren't right. When we lived in Pharr, my daddy would run to the farmer whose land we worked. He would kiss the hand of that man, Mr. Brown. I would be so mad! I would tug at his *calzones*, his long pants of white cloth. I would say no, no, it's not right. I was only small, but I knew that everyone was equal, all alike. My daddy would say, 'You don't know, that could be Cristo Jesús.' I would say, 'Cristo Jesús wouldn't treat you like that and let you kiss his hand!'"

A few years later, on the school bus in Pharr, a group of boys spotted Eva in her long skirt and *rebozo*. They tied her braids to the pole attached to the bus seat, pulled on her hair and chanted, "Wetback, wetback, wetback." That evening, Eva approached her father. "What is it, Daddy, 'wetback'?" Anger wrinkled Fidel's tanned face. He grabbed her hand and ran one finger along the length of her arm. "Look, are you wet?" he shouted. "Are you wet? Are you?" His rage finally subsided. "No, you're not. That's what you tell them. You know who you are."

Eva did know who she was—a truth seeker. By age eleven, she would finish school in the afternoon and drive her mother into Reynosa. Conchita never learned to drive; she reasoned that since Eva could ride a horse, she could master the truck. Eva would perch on top of pillows in the cab of the old pickup to reach the steering wheel. Their excursions included trips into the *colonias* on the edge of Pharr. These unincorporated subdivisions lacked water, sewage, and other municipal services. Built in the 1950s on floodplains and other lands useless for agriculture, they housed the poorest immigrants. Often Eva's mother sold items like bits of fabric or combs, for which she had paid a quarter. "But she would want a dollar for them," Eva says, still outraged. "I would just come right out and say, 'Ma, you only paid a quarter! Why do you want a dollar?' When we got home, she would shout, 'You don't

say that in front of people!' 'Then when do you say it?' I asked.
All those things got me the fame of being mean and being *la mula*.
But I knew it was the truth."

As Eva grew up, she discovered how complex truth could be.
"To me, my daddy was magic," she says. "I still think he was the
only person who truly loved me for what and who I am. He would
stand me in front of him as a little girl, you know, with my little
huaraches that weren't even whole. He just looked at me in my eyes
and said I was beautiful. I knew deep in my heart, it was planted
in me that I was beautiful." But Eva's father was violent toward
her mother, sister, and brothers. She says, "When little Fidel, my
brother, was born, my mom made a gunnysack bag tied up to a
rope on the ceiling for a crib. When the baby cried, my dad would
get up in the night and would grab that little baby by the legs like
he wanted to squash him on the wall. That was worse than if he
had hit me. I carry those scars in my heart."

Those scars forged Eva's ability to live with contradictions, to
perceive light amid shadows. "Even among the drunkenness, the
beatings of my mom and my siblings, he did wonderful things for
people," Eva muses on her father. "My parents got together, and
they both knew so much about healing and everything. They had
something to do, something good for the world, maybe even at the
cost of themselves."

The knots at the center of Eva's family enlarged her vision. Her
testimonios bear witness to similar suffering in the lives of others: women who endure violence, men whose anger leads back to
centuries of colonization, children who join gangs to belong somewhere. Eva never accepts injustice in her life or the lives of others.
But she digs for the roots of violence in poverty and oppression,
exploring how individual pain connects to collective trauma.[3]

Eva ends her memories of growing up by saying, "This is the beautiful story of my childhood, but it's also the horrid story of my childhood." Sadness lingers in her face when she remembers her isolation as a child or the boys who wrapped her braids around the bus pole. When she ponders poverty in the *colonias*, she recalls the times when her own family had no food. She once told me, "When I remember childhood, I can smell and taste it—hunger and the flour tortilla aroma." Living at the edge of poverty, though, pushed *la mula* outward, to uncover the sources of inequality. At the end of the story of *el patron* Mr. Brown, Eva said, "I was so mad at my daddy for kissing Mr. Brown's hand." After a pause, she added, "But I was even madder at Mr. Brown for letting him do it."

5

The Dress That Doesn't Fit

La Enfermedad: If you're hungry, you cannot
think. You even think that there's no God.
Why does everyone else have a lot and I have
nothing? Is God only for some people?

El Remedio: You know it's not just "Peace be with
you" in church. No, peace be with you every
day. And what am I doing to bring you peace?

DRIVING ACROSS THE MOUNTAINS to see Eva in 1999, I follow a Greyhound Bus crammed with travelers—a reminder of a
trip I'd made years before on a similar bus. What I had thought
would be a stress-reducing journey turned out to be a slow crawl
through the Columbia River Gorge, the Blue Mountains, and a
dozen tiny Oregon towns. A wizened woman next to me snored,
mouth open, through much of the trip; the couple behind me
reeked of liquor. I lamented not driving. When I finally arrived at
Eva's, I vowed never to journey by bus again.

This time, a leisurely drive brings me to Nyssa by nightfall. The next morning, we sit and talk as Eva grinds chilies for salsa. Her second daughter, Maria, arrives with her one-year-old, Xochitl, who trails oxygen tubes behind her. Xochitl's black curls and delicate features mirror in miniature her stunning mother. Maria, weighed down by medical paraphernalia, wears a slim floral skirt, heels, and stockings; her long ebony hair is curled. Eva tells me that they nicknamed her "Coco" when she was young for Coco Chanel. "She was so beautiful and always preening!"

Eva calls Xochitl the "miracle child." She was born with severe pulmonary hypertension, one lung and one kidney. Doctors doubted she would live for a year. In Nahuatl, her name means "flower," thereby linking her to her ancestors' poetic tradition of *in xóchitl in cuícatl—flor y canto* (flower and song). The "secret, the hidden," wrote the poet-king Nezahualcóyotl, is that "we all will have to go away/we all will have to die on earth/Like a painting/we will be erased/Like a flower/we will dry up/here on earth."[1] In her beloved granddaughter, Eva sees life's fragility and the need for daily celebration.

Xochitl claps and sputters sounds. "Blow kisses," Maria coaxes, and the baby raises her hands to her mouth. Maria laughs at her daughter's antics, then turns to ask Eva, "Are you coming to church with us?" Eva shakes her head, "No, Catholicism is a dress that doesn't fit me anymore." Maria shrugs and gathers Xochitl's belongings to make the nine o'clock mass at St. Bridget's.

When did the dress fit, I wonder, and what connects the dress to faith? While Eva doesn't attend church, she is the most devout person I know. Cutting oranges someone has left in return for healing, Eva says, "I feel that God prepares you for all you're going to go through. He's not dumb. He gives us every day what we're going to need. He puts it in our bag." What we need, for this day or any other, Eva says as she heats tortillas on her *comal*, is bread and faith. She watches Maria carry Xochitl to the car, then adds, "What does faith taste of? Tea? Raspberries? I think faith can only be lived. It's up to each one of us, not the Church."

Bread and faith—the foundations of Eva's life. When her family lived in Pharr, her father made fifty cents a day on the farm. But two or three times a week, he would look out for the undocumented workers crossing the Rio Grande. "My dad would get up on the roof, 'Hey, did you eat today? Come here!' I would get really angry and say, 'What the hell is he doing? Those people are going to eat all our tortillas.' But you know, we never lacked. My dad would say, '*Dios nos dará más*,' God will give us more."

Eva's parents were "very, very Catholic," raised to be members of special religious societies. Her father belonged to Valle de Santiago's Adorador de Cristo, her mother to Hijas de María. But, Eva stresses, "They had faith by their deeds, not just their words." After they crossed over to the United States, the family couldn't attend church in Pharr. "We were wetbacks, and you don't go places," Eva says. "We used to worship at home and have our own services. Our holy communion was a piece of tortilla with water or juice. My daddy, tears were coming out of his eyes because he said he wasn't worthy of doing this, but there was no other way. He didn't want to lose the ritual of mass, you know. They didn't let it go."

The Protestant church workers who urged Eva's family to send her to school also sought the family's conversion. One day a group of Methodists came to the Browns' farm to invite them to Sunday school. Eva asked her father if it was allowed. "He said 'Yes, you should go because they give you clothes, they give you shoes, they take you out for ice cream. We can't do that and they can. So you do it. Go and sing your head off. God would say it's good.'"

Although Eva's family did not convert, in the last few decades, a growing number of Mexicans have joined other Christian churches. In 2005, 7 percent of Mexicans identified as Protestant. In a 2007 survey, 19.6 percent of Latinos in the United States described themselves as evangelical or born-again Protestants. The count may be higher, given the number of undocumented workers. Many Latinos say that the evangelical music and joyous forms of worship draw them. Pentecostal churches also provide help with job searches, tutoring, and translation.[2] Eva affirms that other denominations sometimes meet needs not addressed by the Catholic Church. "Those other churches, many of them don't only satisfy your soul, but they also look after your body. It's wonderful that other religions do things that our church—I still claim it—is not doing."

"I am a Catholic; I will always be one," Eva says. She is not the only one to "still claim" Catholic identity while not attending mass. The U.S. Church hierarchy complains about the lax church attendance of many Mexican Americans. Mexican Catholicism is a "self-reliant" religious tradition, evolved to meet community needs.[3] Perhaps people don't go to mass, but they remain deeply pious in daily life.

At Eva's, every room overflows with the bright icons, candles, and colors of an *altarcito*, or little altar. She once told her friend, teacher, and scholar, Gabriella Ricciardi, that "everything is an altar, your life is an altar."[4] The altar in Eva's living room features statues of Jesus Christ and the Virgin, but Eva, ever ecumenical, adds a Ganesh from Hindu tradition. To one side stands the statue of El Santo Niño de Atocha that her mother brought from Mexico and gave to Eva before she died. The saint, always portrayed as a small Spanish pilgrim boy, is said to perform miracles in the face of drought and natural disasters. Eva tells a story about when her father was foreman on the Browns' farm in charge of the water supply. Once, he fell asleep and the water inundated a neighbor's farm. Fidel Silva awoke, then frantically tried to fix the extensive damage. He felt he was doomed, but he prayed to El Santo Niño de Atocha. The next day, the land appeared untouched but for a child's footprints.

Central to Eva's pantheon is the brown-skinned Virgin of Guadalupe. Her image saturates the Guadalupe Room in Eva's house where guests often sleep. To many Latinos, she is known simply as "La Virgen." According to the frequently told story, she appeared in 1531 to a poor Aztec, Juan Diego, on the hill of Tepeyac in Mexico. Speaking Nahuatl, the Virgin sent Juan Diego to the archbishop to ask that a church be built on the hill. Her request was completed only after she effected a miracle: Juan Diego's gathering of roses supernaturally flowering in the desert and the imprinting of her image onto his cloak. In pre-Hispanic times, indigenous people had journeyed to Tepeyac to pay homage to the fertility goddess, Tonantzin. Christianized Mexicans grafted the powerful symbol of Guadalupe onto existing beliefs and practices. Mexicans continued to syncretize Tonantzin and Guadalupe until the seventeenth century, when Spanish friars discouraged the "wicked" worship of the goddess. The cult of Guadalupe, encouraged by the Church, blossomed. Now she appears in restaurants and bullrings, taxis and trucks, at political marches and on home altars. She is the symbol of hope, of the Indian and the mestizo, the one image capable of melding the multiple strains of Mexican and Mexican American identity.[5] But as a symbol for women, Guadalupe is complex. Her downcast eyes and hands folded in prayer belie the strength women attribute to her. Her real power is latent, waiting to be tapped. Eva's deep attraction to La Virgen mirrors her contradictory relationship with the Church and its rules for women. Under her Guadalupe hovers the spirit of Tonantzin.

The melding of the indigenous goddess and the Virgin mirrors the broader synthesis of Mexican Catholicism. During the Spanish colonization in the 1500s, the Nahuatl wise men—the *tlamatinime*—stood before Cortés and the Spanish friars and declared, "If, as you say, our gods are dead, it is better that you allow us to die, too."[6] But the culture did not die. Some indigenous beliefs and practices went underground; others merged with Catholic symbols and practices. Throughout the Southwest, beliefs and practices of Native Americans add to this already complex mix. All of it influenced Eva's version of Catholicism and the creation of a dress that fits.

To fit, the garment must be ample and flexible. As we clean up the kitchen after breakfast, Eva describes some of her anger at the Church's rigidity. She recounts the story of one granddaughter who had to forego the church component of her *quinceañera*. Had she completed the required religious preparation, she would have been seventeen by the time she could celebrate her fifteenth birthday. "I may put it on," she says of the dress, "but I won't look and feel good."

Eva also acknowledges her long engagement with the Church. For many years, she and Ted were involved with Marriage Encounter. The program is now offered through a variety of religious groups, but it began as a Catholic marriage renewal process to create mutual respect and open communication. Eva and Ted tried to strengthen their relationship and help others. The Church in Oregon also played a pivotal role in aiding migrants. In 1955, the Portland Archdiocese established its Migrant Ministry, which turned into the Oregon Friends of Migrants in 1964 and eventually became the Valley Migrant League (VML). The VML organized progressive clergy, politicians, employers, and workers to obtain grants for migrant vocational training, day care, health care, and other services. Change began in Oregon's Willamette Valley but spread across the state. In 1965, Treasure Valley Community College in Ontario set up a similar program.[7]

Eva draws a line between actions motivated by institutional requirements and those that spring from love. In the 1980s, she received a grant from the Baker Diocese to study theology and sociology at Portland State University. "I got the grant," she said, "because I was really involved. I wasn't involved because I was religious; I was involved because I love people. I was involved because I love kids. I don't know what 'religious' means; I do not know how faith looks. I would get together here with fifty or sixty teenagers and make dances for them. I got together to teach the children songs and teach them that there's this great spirit that helps you. I hung around with couples that were troubled or hurt, because I had been."

Catholic rituals remain essential to Eva. To those who convert, she says, "If you want to move to another religion where there are no rites of passage, go ahead." Ritual and rites of passage are the warp and weft of Mexican Catholicism. Imagine the year beginning with El Día de Los Reyes (the Epiphany) on January 6. You might find a tiny statue of Cristo Jesús in your Rosca de Reyes, an oval sweet bread decorated with candied fruit. Such good luck makes you the host for the February 2 celebration of Candelaria, or Candlemass Day. Soon, preparations begin for Lenten fast-ing, then Semana Santa—the holy week festivals that precede the grand celebration of Easter. Mother's Day follows, then harvest festivals and the all-night graveyard vigils and offerings to Los Muertos on November 1 and 2. La Virgen de Guadalupe's celebration on December 12 leads into Christmas Posadas that re-create Mary and Joseph's search for lodging before the birth of Christ. Time remains suspended while rituals are enacted, each passage enlivened by parades in the streets, mariachi bands, songs of joy and death, prayers chanted and wept. Sandwiched between these yearly rituals are dozens of formal and informal pilgrimages. Some follow paths to shrines such as the Basilica of Our Lady of San Juan del Valle, which I visited with Eva; others journey to sites of less official folk saints. Don Pedrito Jaramillo in south Texas and El Niño Fidencio in Espinazo, Mexico—both *curanderos* during their lifetimes—are the most famous. *Papel picado*, masks, wax flowers, and other folk arts brighten many rituals; the somber light of candles illuminates others.

Rituals also activate *compadrazgo*, the extended kinship system that links families and their resources. The *compadre* (literally "coparent") relationship between parents and godparents (padrinos) often begins when a child is baptized. The *compadre* and *comadre* continue to support the child financially and emotionally through the Holy Communion, *quinceañera*, wedding, and other life markers. In some communities, multiple individuals and couples become sponsors for different rites of passage. Traditionally, the godmother and godfather (the *padrino* and *madrina*) also step in if something happens to the biological parents. The *padrinos* ensure the child's Catholic upbringing, education, and growth into a responsible citizen.[8] In the United States, the meaning of *comadres* and *compadres* has expanded to include close friends. Eva has many *comadres* who are important to her, women she might ask to bring food to an event. For while the soul needs ritual, the body craves *menudo* and *barbacoa* and, always, tortillas. Bread and faith.

After Maria and her daughter depart, I ask Eva how she has sustained her faith in the face of Xochitl's fragile health. Her response once again links faith and healing to the earth. Eva describes watching her mother heal people who came to their farm in Pharr. She used herbs and plants and the strength of her belief. "She would say, 'God will give me the strength. God will give me the way.' This woman raised people out of beds where doctors said, 'No more.' At least three that I truly saw and know of because of faith, the faith that she infused into people because she had it. And not only words, you know, but deeds. That's where I got it [faith]. From them, not from the Church."

Perhaps stories of the earth prompt Eva's announcement that she has planned a journey out of town for our Sunday together. "Where?" I ask. "It's a miracle," Eva replies. "There are miracles everywhere." I don't know if she refers to her mother's healing, to Xochitl's life, or to a place in the mountains she is determined to show me. "Wait until you see it," she declares.

In late morning, we rattle along in Eva's old Continental, past the wheat and onion fields toward the Owyhee Mountains, about seventy-five miles southeast of Nyssa. As the red rock cliffs rise around us, Eva grows more exuberant about our destination. "It's so beautiful!" We turn off onto a winding mountain road, ascend a gravel path, and park. Beyond an incline treacherous with loose rock stands a fence topped by barbed wire. Eva crawls under the wire. I follow. We climb toward a long row of dark clay mounds lining the edge of the dun-colored cliff. Into the center of one, a swallow disappears. Breathless, Eva beams at me, "The Swallows' Castle! Isn't it amazing?" She describes her first visit here, how she watched the mountain's rough edges transform with the swallows' arrival. The burnt red of the Owyhee Valley unfolds beneath us, a striking contrast to the miniature wonder of the castles. We perch and watch the tiny birds flit back and forth into their shelters. "Amazing," I agree. Yet, I feel oddly deflated. What had I expected? I can't tell Eva that I had anticipated something more spectacular than the mounds of small brown creatures.

The words "*te quiero*" awaken me in the Guadalupe Room on Sunday night. Passion from a telenovela steams up the living room, punctuated by real voices and the sound of a woman crying. Two young women have joined Eva on the couch: I see them when I stumble into the bathroom, then return to bed. The next day I learn that these young lesbians came from a nearby migrant camp to escape harassment by male workers. They can't find refuge in the Catholic Church, but Eva offers both religious and secular solace. "The Lord teaches us what we need to know. Not to judge. If you do this or that, that's okay because God made you. But if you're homosexual or lesbian, our Church doesn't want you." Years later, Eva will officiate at a wedding of two young women in Boise. She will be proud that she can help celebrate a ritual that she considers deeply spiritual. She will remain unconcerned that the Church and State do not recognize this union. What matters, Eva says, is that love is pure.

Monday night, Maria returns after work. She leaves Xochitl with Eva and me while she visits her brother Diego, who lives a few blocks away. We play with the baby outside, laughing at how she waves her arms with the oxygen tubes tangled behind her. But

after Maria picks up Xochitl and departs, Eva gets very quiet. I
remember a sweltering day in July when I asked Eva how she could
bear Nyssa's insistent heat. "I sit very still," she said. Eva's still-
ness is also spiritual; it quells her anxiety about how long beautiful
Xochitl might survive. Eva's life is a minute-by-minute devotion—
a living flower song. Now, she looks to El Santo Niño de Atocha
on her altar just before she breaks down. "They say there's no hope
for Xochitl. They cannot replace the heart or the lungs without
threatening one or the other. My doctor says not to worry or get
stressed, but I have a granddaughter who might not live."

We move to the couch. Eva switches on the telenovelas as she
weaves together the threads of our conversation. "Being close to
God," she says, "doesn't mean that you're not going to have any
problems; I think that's when you have more. But you're guided to
know that there is a way." The talk of God mixed with Mexican
soap operas seems odd, even irreverent. But the human struggles
central to the overblown telenovelas are occasions for faith; even—
perhaps especially—here, Eva finds "the God I wait for," as she
does in every person she encounters. She says, "You know, for a
time religion to me was just the Catholic Church. Go to church.
'Genoveva Castellanoz, católica [Catholic]. I was a person with
a last name that is Catholic. Later, it became love. Now, I love."

A few days later, on my return drive out of Nyssa, I pass the Greyhound bus departing for Portland. I think back to my own bus
journey years before. Eva drove me to Ontario the morning of my
departure. We ate breakfast at Denny's near the entrance ramp for
I-84, traffic roaring beneath us. Back on the bus, I surveyed the
seat choices. Everyone smelled bad or looked menacing. I finally
sat next to a man whose white ponytail curled down onto the box

6

Choosing Ripeness

La Enfermedad: It's not good to pluck a plum
that's just tiny, which is what I was.

El Remedio: Along the way, I thought, "If God ever
gave me little girls, they would know [about their
bodies]. I was going to give the freedom to my
daughters that was denied me for being a woman."

ON THE PICNIC TABLE on Eva's back patio sit two large garden tomatoes. One bursts with plump ripeness, its deep red illuminated by sunlight through the locust tree. The other remains
hard and green. We're pretending: I am the young girl choosing
flowers for the *corona* I will wear for my *quinceañera*. Eva places
a worn hand with a single long thumbnail on the green fruit, "I
talk to young girls and young men. First, I have them taste this
one, then the ripe one. Which is better? They know. I say, 'Life is
the same. And it will be better when you are older, when the time
comes.'" I could be any one of the hundreds of young women who

have come to Eva for advice and a *corona* during the decade that
I've known her. I've watched her make the floral crowns, but until
now, I hadn't heard her own story of coming of age. Eva's teachings spring from what she never had—an introduction to adolescence, adulthood, and her own body.

Life on the farm and, for many years, her family's illegal status,
kept Eva isolated. Even at school, her difference—as indigenous,
as a person whose family fed themselves from the dump and sold
chickens—kept her apart. Seeing Eva now, still youthful in a purple T-shirt and jeans, white ankle socks and sandals, I imagine the
adolescent she describes: after school, a slim girl in a long skirt,
braids plaited with banana leaves, walks the road into Pharr with
her mother. The chickens they will peddle to homes and restaurants are slung across their shoulders. Later, she returns to the
fields, then to a small shack by a deep culvert to do homework; she
then rises the next morning to pick onions before school.

I have never seen a photo of her mother, but I can conjure her
through Eva's stories of appreciation and anger. Describing how
Conchita dragged her along to sell chickens, Eva says, "I think
she forgot that I was just a little girl. But you know what? I could
carry them. And we walked to town, about eight or nine miles."
Conchita, Eva says, took excellent care of her daughters, despite
constant back problems and endless work. Yet, her mother's strict
rules caused Eva anguish. Once, "a beautiful boy who played foot-
ball" asked Eva to the prom. "My mom said yes, and she sells this
huge pig to buy my dress. Then, after I was combed and dressed
and bathed and my shoes on, she said for me to walk. She watched
me walk and she said, 'Hmmm. You're not going.'" Embarrassment kept Eva from school for a long time. Speculating now, she
says, "I think my mama didn't know any better, and I think she

was jealous of me. She never loved my daddy, but I did, and he loved me back. Then I think, maybe she was really scared after losing all her children. What love could you have?"

Since Conchita told her daughters nothing about sexuality or reproduction, Eva didn't understand the tingling in her body when she met a young man named Elías at the local gas station. "My heart would just pound and pound." One day, he came to Eva's homeroom at school and invited her to walk to the water fountain. "I was speechless but I could nod my head. So we went and came back and I couldn't think anymore. Later, he takes my hand and walks me to my bus line. I was just on cloud nine, floating. I got home and got dressed to work in the fields. Piggly Wiggly—that's a major store—had ordered seven hundred bunches of onions. I go out, and then I feel this terrible pain my stomach, something I had never felt before, a stickiness down there. And oooh, I remember a conversation I'd heard from some older girls only a few days before. I remember these words only: 'When you're with a man for the first time, you bleed.' So I go into the weeds and look at my panties. Redder than red! Oooh, my God. Elías held my hand and look what happened! So I went on picking onions, went home, and got into the cold water in the canal. I thought, just stay there as long as you can and see if it goes away. My mom never told me and I got the wrong information and I suffered so much."

I bite the ripe tomato as Eva laughs at her adolescent naïveté. But under high spirits lingers her pain. We move from the patio to the casita—past the zinnias and sunflowers—accompanied by the cockatiel's screech. Inside, the shelves buckle under rolls of ribbon, multicolored tissue paper, wax to be melted in an old wok, pipe cleaners, and other supplies for creating *coronas*. Since Eva received the National Heritage Award from the National Endowment for the Arts in 1989, people have flocked to her. She doesn't accept money for the *coronas*; like healing, they are gifts to the community. They also fulfill one of Eva's childhood longings.

Growing up, Eva wanted to be an artist or a dancer as well as a poet. Her father dismissed such activities as work "for prostitutes." In her *mula* fashion, Eva found her path toward art through making *coronas*. "I believe in falling in love at first sight. That's the most wonderful love, and *coronas* to me were that." Eva had never seen a *corona* as a child, and didn't have one for her own *quinceañera*. "Mine happened at home. We were scared that Immigration was going to catch us and send us back, so we couldn't go to church. My mom made my wreath. It didn't have any flowers; it only had weeds, a vinelike thing that grew along the ditch where we lived. That's all I had, just a branch of it intertwined with others. My momma made a special turkey, a white turkey because they were very symbolic people."

After Eva and Ted married, they went to Guadalajara for her to meet his family. On the street, a man with a cart dipped paper flowers into hot wax to form *coronas*. "He had this can with a wick and petroleum. I watched him and asked what he was doing. I thought I could do it, too, so I brought it back in my heart." At first, Eva worried about how she could buy supplies. She needed paper, wax, and wire to shape the flowers, a container to melt the wax to 120 degrees—simple needs, but requiring money she didn't have. But she found crayons at school and old candles at yard sales. The first attempts "weren't pretty," but they steadily improved.

Now, Eva stashes boxes of flowers throughout her casita. She saves them in part because "the flowers are alive. I love to see them being born," she says. They are part of the universe of "things that do not speak" from which she learns profound lessons. From

under a bed, Eva removes a special *corona* to show me. Its flowers are crude and less realistic than her now more polished work;
another white flower with twisted leaves testifies to darker times.
One day, she was shaping a *corona* when her sister came in, her
face ashen. Their father's bone cancer had just been diagnosed.
"The doctor said Daddy has been sick this way for more than forty
years. They had X-rayed his whole body and it was black. When I
sat down and went back to my work, my flowers had teeth. They
were mad. And I saved them." The darker flowers, too, are part of
a tradition "too beautiful to die," Eva says, because "the flowers
tell a story of a people."

Here is how Eva relates that story:

A young woman arrives to prepare for the *quinceañera*. She
chooses from the styles Eva has laid out—crowns with light green
or pink buds tucked in between the *azahares*, the tiny white flowers that mimic orange blossoms. Eva wants the young woman to
carry with her the message about chastity and the importance of
finishing school before she marries. Soon, the young woman will
be barraged by choices. Will she wear her *corona* on a diadema
or tiara? Should she choose a white dress or a pastel color? Gifts
from godparents and friends will include jewelry and a *medalla de
oro*—a religious gold medal, often of the Virgin of Guadalupe—
to be worn during the church ceremony. The young woman will
carry a *libro y rosario* (missal and rosary) identical to those that
she, not the groom, will later hold as a bride, marking her responsibility for the family's spiritual life. She will recite a prayer to Guadalupe, creating direct links to a Mexican and indigenous past.
After the church service, she might undergo a change of shoes into
high heels or cradle a baby doll given by the godmother—the mark
of her ability to bear children. Then the crowd will move to some-

one's home or community center for a party. The young woman will offer the first dance to her father and perhaps drink alcohol publicly for the first time.[1]

We're en route to a bon marché in Ontario as Eva describes this ideal *quinceañera* process. At the thrift shop, I look for a scarf. Eva hunts for candles to stock her supply cupboard and for items with hummingbirds that she often buys for me. As we wander, she talks about changes to the *quinceañera*. She grows wistful describing how commercial and secular the event has become in the United States. Young girls don't come to her as frequently now. Many prefer rhinestone or glass beads to her carefully detailed *azahares*. Most often, Eva makes *coronas* in libraries and at arts education conferences.

Tracing the *quinceañera's* history is difficult, its origins murky. Most studies cite a mix of indigenous initiation traditions with elements of European balls. The language and practices also evoke American debutante parties. In Eva's day, only the well-heeled had such glitzy parties; most *quinceañeras* were simple, rural events such as hers. Now all is up for grabs, according to Julia Alvarez in her book about the changing *quinceañera*. Today's parties often resemble weddings minus the groom. The young woman is escorted by a *chamberlán* and accompanied by a full court of young men in tuxedos and *damas* in ball gowns. Middle-class and working families save for years to fund elaborate meals, limos. and photos galore. Magazines, shops, and Internet sites dispense *quinceañera* items and advice. For those who can't afford such splendor, Alvarez chronicles an alternative: forego the event and settle for photos. "Only in America," she writes, "a land in part made up of movies, would having a record on celluloid be an alternative to having the actual celebration."[2]

Today's *quinceañera* bends tradition to the demands of modernity. But which way should it lean? Should a young woman incur debt to have her moment of fame in a celebrity-obsessed culture? How is freedom shaped for young women? Eva wanted to enlighten her daughters about sex before they entered adulthood. "I told them as best I could, with embarrassment and what have you. And my girls said, 'Oh, Mama, we know that.'" She wanted her daughters to get to know their boyfriends, so she hid their visits from her husband, Ted. But she also warned them about the consequences of pregnancy. Traditional Mexican culture reveres motherhood, so teenage pregnancy is not stigmatized in the same ways as it is in mainstream American society. Yet, an unmarried pregnant daughter disgraces the family's name. "They blame the mother especially," Eva says. "Ted would say, 'This is not a brothel. If anyone in this house gets pregnant, whoever it is, is going to blah, blah, blah out of this house. This is an honorable house.'"

Eva also stresses that what's good for the goose is good for the gander. At a wedding, the groom should also wear a white *azahare* to represent his chastity. Otherwise, tradition imprisons. Eva rails against the double standard that enslaves girls while giving boys their freedom. Above all, society must value girls equally. "It starts with birth," Eva says. "Our men want boys, boys, boys. This should change now." In raising her sons, she says, "I always thought that I was going to grow my sons, as if they were turkeys, to be the husbands for other women."

Eva believes that culture can liberate by helping young girls stay in school and find their path. She is not alone in using tradition to urge change. In Latino communities throughout the United States, programs have sprung up to help young people negotiate such choices. In Nampa, Idaho, eleven miles east of the Oregon border, Ana Maria Schachtell started the Stay-in-School Quinceañera Program. This project rests at the heart of the Hispanic Cultural Center, which Schachtell lobbied to create after watching her son participate in a *quinceañera* court. Through the center's program, Latino judges, lawyers, and artists speak to young people about possible career paths, counsel them to finish school, and encourage them to embrace their heritage.[3] These goals echo those Eva has pursued throughout her life.

Can one read Eva's teachings and the meaning of her *coronas* through a feminist lens? While I transcribed Eva's stories, I read extensively about the depth and range of Latina feminism. Though Latinas have always fought for social justice, feminist struggle in the United States goes back to the 1930s and '40s. The critical roles Latinas played as labor union organizers generated self-esteem as well as awareness of gender inequality. Women helped mobilize farmworkers, activism that later drew male and female students to *el movimiento*—the Chicano movement of the 1960s and '70s. Despite strong ties to the civil rights community, Latinos had separate goals. "It was not that they wanted a piece of the 'American pie,'" writes Vicki Ruiz. "They wanted the freedom to bake their own *pan dulce* [sweet bread]."[4] *El movimiento* transformed the negative barrio term "Chicano" into a symbol of commitment to social justice. However, Latina feminists bristled when men looked to a utopian nationalist past—part of a history they saw as oppressing women. How could society change if dominated by romantic images of Aztec warriors bent over docile (light-skinned) virgins? Some male members of the Chicano movement labeled Latina feminists "Malinches"—traitors to their group. Malinche, whose full name was Malintzin Tenepal, was the indigenous woman sold into slavery by her family and then given to Hernán Cortés as translator and consort. Latina feminists called for rethinking Malinche's image and for attention to women's needs within the broader Chicano movement.[5]

Latinas also challenged the largely white second wave of feminism. They joined women from varied ethnic and class backgrounds to declare their distinct needs.[6] Latina, African American, Asian American, and other voices fill the 1981 ground-breaking work *This Bridge Called My Back: Writings by Radical Women of Color.* The collection captured the artistic vision and the frustrations of women of color. In the 1980s, other anthologies and journals emerged, many of them inspired by oral histories and the *testimonios* of previously excluded women.

Divisions exist within Latina feminism, just as they do in the broader movement. If Eva called herself a feminist, she might fit into that group of Latina feminists that stresses the well-being of family and community as well as autonomy for women. Her activism stems from her commitment "to make sure what was done to me does not happen to other women." But Eva rejects all labels, including feminist. When she won a National Heritage Award, a friend called to say, "You've been declared a 'National Treasure.'" Eva's response was, "The best name that anyone can give me is 'Woman, Human Being.'"

When we return from Ontario, we rummage through Eva's casita for *coronas* I will take back to Portland for an exhibit. She chooses flowers with the most perfect white *azahares* to represent her artistry. "We are symbol people," Eva says of her family and culture, and white is one of her key symbols. Promoting purity may seem to support the control of women and thus contradictory to liberation. "The master's tools will never dismantle the master's house," wrote feminist poet Audre Lorde.[7] But sometimes the cultural tools we receive are the only ones we have for transformation. Eva twists the meaning of white to promote equal sexuality and power, but within marriage. Like most ideals, it is one not always realized. When young people stumble, including her own children, she does not judge them. She says, "I am not a judge. I am not a jury. I am not God. I am the most imperfect of all." Tradition is a tool, not a moral bludgeon.

The meaning of a symbol rests on what is not expressed as well as on what is. Perhaps it's logical that Eva exalts white, for through its symbolism she promotes what she never had: knowledge about her body and the freedom to shape her destiny. Nowhere would the power of this symbol be more evident than at her wedding.

7

Gnawing the Bone

La Enfermedad: When I got married, my mom put on
La Sal, which is done when somebody wishes you
bad. My daddy said that if I found meat, I should
eat it. If I found bone, I should sit down and gnaw it
because he didn't want me crying at his doorstep.

El Remedio: I had done such a bad thing by eloping, I
was not allowed to wear a white dress. Why should
I wear a blue dress? This is not right. Traditions are
good, but the ones that are not good, choke them!

ON THE AFTERNOON OF JUNE 24, 1955, Eva stood in
front of St. Margarita's Catholic Church on Hawk Street in Pharr,
Texas. Teodoro Castellanoz, her husband-to-be, waited inside for
her to approach the altar with her father. Her mother, Conchita,
did not attend the wedding. Eva wore a sky-blue ankle-length
gown. She was fifteen years old.

On a fine October day in 2001, Eva and I stand in the same spot on Hawk Street. The week before, we drove south on Highway 281 to her daughter Chayo's house in Pharr. I kept the tape recorder perched on the console between us as Eva described the events leading up to the formal ceremony that followed her "elopement."

"I was not interested in men," Eva says of her teenage years, having grown frustrated by her mother's clamp on her romantic possibilities. "I just worked and escaped into study and books." But men, including Teodoro Castellanoz, watched Eva as she tended her father's horses and worked the bean fields. Though her father always told her she was beautiful, in the tangle of adolescence Eva felt, "I wasn't pretty—or was made to believe I wasn't. I had long, long hair. I was always barefoot. I rode horseback to take care of the cattle. I just loved to make the horses fly, and my hair would just fly out. Nobody could pry me off that horse."

One day, a man stopped Eva to say that Ted had been watching her and wanted to be her *novio* (boyfriend). "I said, 'Well, I don't even know him.' So he says, 'Well, he's going to be under the mesquite tree when you go by.'" When Eva saw Ted—a "just gorgeous" man in a leather cap and jacket—she knew. This would be her entry into the clique of older girls who had ignored her as an *india*. Ted sent her a picture, which she proudly displayed at school. But Eva stresses, "I was not in love." With an echo from her parents' marriage, she asks, "How can you love someone you don't know?"

Conchita and Fidel Silva already had someone in mind for Eva and for her sister, Gorda—the sons of Don Claudio, another Mexican worker who lived near the farm. Though her parents rarely socialized, they had long visited with Don Claudio's family to create ties for the future. "They wanted Ricardo and Luis for me and my sister. We all grew up together. But in my heart, being *la mula* that I was probably since I was born, that was not going to happen. To me, Ricardo was my brother. We'd bathed together since we were children."

I heard many of these stories before on my visits to Eva's home in Oregon, but during our week together in Pharr, they take on the resonant details of the landscape. Before arriving at St. Margarita's that morning, we drove past prickly pear cacti and stands of mesquite trees. Eva pointed out the spot close to where Ted had waited for her that afternoon many years before. He also sent Eva love notes in which he pleaded for her to slip out of the house at night. She responded by letter that she would never do that. When he appeared below her window one moonlit night, Eva held back. "My mother had talked to me like a mother should. She said we didn't know Ted, maybe he was married in Mexico; she probably knew things because she dealt with a lot of people as a healer." Though Eva resisted her parents' plans for an arranged marriage, she respected their notions of tradition. To remain a virgin, to be married in a white dress with a ring on your finger, was to be a respectable woman. "We were poor, we were wetbacks, but I wanted it." Though she yearned for these traditional life passages, Eva said, "I would be the *mula*." She kept scribbling notes to Ted. When her father discovered them, he exploded. Any contact with a man could be construed as something more. "When he found out, he hit me. I had never spoken to a man, I had never touched a man, I had never nothing a man." Eva's mother had to cut her clothes off after the beating. Later, Ted said of her father's violence, "People don't even do that to animals."

Ted unleashed his own anger. When Eva resisted his advances, he started circling her schoolyard at lunchtime in his car. He threatened to *robar* (steal) her from her family. Eva told him she didn't want to marry him. "But I was really scared of him taking me away. I would see my little brothers and sister and think, 'What if I don't get to see them anymore? What if he takes me to Mexico?' You're a little girl, you don't know! You don't know anything. But I was scared of my dad, of what he had done. I ran away with Ted because I didn't want to be taken by force."

As we stand in front of St. Margarita's, Eva describes why she agreed to "being stolen." She says, "They call it 'stealing' or *robar* when they do it this way, but nobody steals you. You go willingly—you run behind the man! Ted told me the day and the time. You're taken to a relative or a friend's house that you trust. Ted did it right because he didn't take me to his house. He took me to our *padrino* and our *madrina*. That is called *depositar*; they deposit you at the home. You are not seen by the groom until the wedding. Everything is worked through the people where he deposits you, those are going to be the *padrinos* at the wedding."

While Eva was being "deposited" at the home of Dr. Godines, Ted's *padrino*, another drama unfolded across town. Eva's mother was searching for her at Don Claudio's. Eva had lied to her for several months, pretending Ricardo was her boyfriend. When her parents discovered Eva was with Ted, disgrace seemed inevitable. Marrying Ted would muddy the family name, as would not marrying him. Ted had threatened her with this possibility, Eva recalls. "He said, 'If I want to, I'll marry you, and if I don't, I won't.' See, that would have been a greater disgrace for my family and for my dad." Tradition trapped them all. The gleaming church seems benign as Eva continues her story. But the power of the past still reverberates for her. "They were fighting for me," she says of her parents. To try to force Ted to marry Eva, they had him arrested, since she was a minor. But once Ted began the *depositar*, he was released.

Eva emphasizes the differences between her experience and her mother's. "I wasn't stolen like my mama was stolen," she stresses. "I followed Ted." Later, when I hunt for information about the tradition of *robar*, I find documentation of Aztec marriage practices that include "pseudo-abduction." A mock denigration of the young woman occurred in the company of both families until the girl's parents finally consented; she was then carried off to the home of the groom-to-be's relatives and applauded in the streets.[1] This practice seems closest to the dramatic "theft" of the bride that Eva describes, one still enacted in some Mexican and Mexican American communities.

Other accounts of *robar* include darker interpretations. In 2003, older women in Jalisco told of being carried off at gunpoint as recently as the 1960s. Sometimes, the man raped the woman so she would be forced to marry him and save the family's honor. The women used the term *llevar* (to carry off) as well as *robar*.[2] The custom's roots lie in colonial Mexico, where boundaries got blurred between socially arranged marriages, coerced unions, and rape. Throughout the eighteenth and nineteenth centuries, victims were often forced to marry their rapist. Spanish elites charged that "morally weak" Indians perpetuated this pattern. In fact, it crossed ethnic and class lines and derived from Spanish rather than indigenous custom.[3]

There is no such violence in Eva's story of her mother being "taken" from her grandmother's porch in Valle de Santiago. Yet, Eva makes clear that her parents did not honor the ritual dimension of *robar*—the aspect of traditional culture that is essential for her. "My dad just took my mom home to live with someone she didn't even know," she says. "He didn't even deposit her! I always thought that was wrong." Once again, Eva uncovers the hypocrisy of demanding that she conform to tradition while others are not held to the same standard.

After the *depositar*, Eva and Ted held their formal wedding at St. Margarita's, minus the white dress. Eva returned to her parents' home to pick up her belongings. Conchita forbade her from taking anything. "She was so mad," Eva said. "She put on *la sal* [Mexican Spanish meaning both 'salt' and 'bad luck or misfortune'], which is done when somebody wishes you bad. She said that God wasn't going to even help me get salt to eat an avocado. When this comes from your mother, well, that is the very end. I had done such a bad thing by eloping. To my father, it was very, very awful what I did. It was better to them how they did it. I couldn't wear a white dress. We were married at St. Margarita's Church at about three o'clock. My dress was beautiful, super-gorgeous—sky blue, ankle length. After all the mumbo-jumbo that went with it, it was over, my daddy said that if I found meat, I should eat it. If I found bone, I should sit down and gnaw it because he didn't want me crying at his doorstep."

Eva's parents moved to west Texas after her wedding. They fled the Browns' farm and the life they knew because of the shame brought by Eva's actions. "That made me feel like a dog. I had done the wrongest of wrongs; I had disgraced them." Eva's family would eventually accept her back. But immediately following the wedding, she entered the sphere of her husband's family. "After I got married, our *padrinos* took us to Ted's house, a tin little house on the farm. Gifts were waiting for us there. Mrs. Brown and her daughters, and other white people that they knew, had bought us sheets, plates, and household things." Eva often says of her husband, "Ted has always tried to do the best that he can in the material way."

As we leave St. Margarita's, Eva says, "He is still my husband, Ted. We are linked by marriage." Despite the difficulties she's faced in this partnership, the bond remains. I think back to the *lazos* (bonds) I've seen in her casita. Eva makes these wedding headpieces that symbolically link bride and groom. She uses satin as well as wax and paper for the flowers. She didn't have one for her ceremony, but she considers them a critical teaching tool. "When weddings come up," she says, "I make sure to get into what's maybe not my business. But a woman is my business because I am a woman, I have daughters, I have granddaughters who are going to grow up and get a husband. I try to get both the man and the woman and I say, 'Do you know what the *lazo* means?' It's two circles; they are equal. One is not bigger than the other one. It's fifty-fifty—fifty you, fifty me."

Eva's life centers on rituals and rites of passage, but she will remake or jettison those that are not life-enhancing. "Traditions to me are very, very important. My parents instilled them in me but in a few instances with a double standard. As I was standing at St. Margarita's, waiting for the priest, I thought 'Why am I wearing a blue dress?' Because of what my parents had told me? This is not right, because your life is at stake. It shouldn't keep hurting until you're sixty-two. No! You should be able to look back and be proud. Traditions are good, but the ones that are not good, choke them!"

As we circle back to Chayo and Ricardo's, the sun plunges, streaking crimson across the sky. Eva turns to me suddenly, her face backlit by the slanting rays. "I tell my daughters," she says, "'I will have my white dress when I die.' It's put away in a little box. I will have it. I deserve that white dress." Describing the secret box, Eva's mouth sets between a smile and a grimace. I remember how

8

The Door and the Hinge

La Enfermedad: I still don't have the husband
that my kids needed. I wanted it like my
blouse. I wanted it to fit. My husband was
too big; I wanted to cut him to size.

El Remedio: My husband cannot give me all of
happiness; it starts with me. I need a partner
like a door needs a hinge, but it's still a door,
and even without the hinge, it still can close.

THE PHOTO TAKES MY BREATH AWAY: a young Eva, her
heart-shaped face softer and fuller than now, the cheekbones less
pronounced. Clear, dark eyes gaze out above a half smile. Her
hair flows in waves past simple white earrings; embroidered flowers climb up the sides of a white sweater with covered buttons.
Beside her is Ted, thick black hair sloping to a widow's peak that
mirrors the furrow between heavy brows. His unsmiling mouth
seems more determined than unhappy. He is the song of experi-

ence, she of innocence. Seeing them side-by-side, I imagine Ted falling in love with the young girl whose hair mimicked the mane of the horses as she flew across the Browns' farm. I see how Ted's smoldering intensity drew Eva to the grown-up looking man who wore a leather cap and jacket.

"I don't recognize her," Eva says of her former self as we settle down to Chinese takeout. We're at the home of Chana, Eva's youngest daughter, and her husband Luis, called "Brown" for his dark skin. They have returned to Nyssa after several years as store managers in California, and are now once again part of Castellanoz family meals. Their rented house sits across from the seed factory at the edge of town. Plaster of paris cherubs, birds, lions, and other animals enliven the interior—treasures from the bon marchés Chana frequents with Eva. A large antique wooden table dominates the dining room. The composition at meals depends on who is in town, and available. Many nights, Eva's children are working night shift at the Amalgamated Sugar Factory or at a school meeting or athletic match. Tonight, it will be Eva, me, Chana, Brown, and one of their daughters, Lola. Another daughter, Punky, is in Arizona, married and about to have her second child. Blonde, blue-eyed Priscilla, Eva's daughter-in-law, whose husband Marty is in Iraq, soon joins us.

Driving over the night before, beyond the long dip of Farewell Bend, I anticipated the renewal a visit with Eva always brings. Part of that rejuvenation comes from temporary inclusion in her kinlike web. Other friends tell me they feel this, too. Eva has enfolded many outsiders into meals and celebrations with her ever-expanding clan of nine children, their children and grandchildren, *compadres*, and other nonbiological family.

In the early years of Eva's marriage, Ted helped maintain this

extended network. He and Eva took in a boy whose mother had
been murdered. Their family was one of the first to host Mexican
and Latin American exchange students who came to Nyssa High
School. Once, they found three men in the fields "half dead from
hunger. From hunger—in this country!" Eva adds for emphasis.
"We sheltered them and kept them for a long time. We were never
alone; we always shared our house." Ted provided well in material
ways in their early marriage. "He was a very good worker," Eva
says. "People were glad to have him, and lucky to get him." But for
years, Eva has been on her own. I've only met Ted once. Nearly a
decade ago, he arrived in an eighteen-wheeler he was driving for
work, sleeping in the cab at night. This still-handsome man was
and remains a phantom figure, fading in and out of Eva's life.

I've known Eva for over a dozen years, but the photo at Chana's
house is the first I've seen of her as a young woman. Photos were a
luxury, especially in a migratory life. Now, I can't take my eyes off
the dual portrait. "You're so beautiful together," I say. Eva smiles
and then tells me a story. Mike Midlo, the producer of "Oregon
Artbeat" for Oregon Public Broadcasting, came to Nyssa just
weeks before to interview Eva about her *coronas*. "When he saw
the photo of me and Ted, I said 'Just cut out that other half of the
picture.'" We laugh at the collision of Eva's reality and my roman-
ticism. I watch Chana carefully. Her long auburn hair drawn into
a knot reveals a soft, heart-shaped face much like her mother's in
her youth. Chana laughs, but I suspect her mirth is hard won. Her
eyes can blaze, as do those of Eva's other daughters, at the mention of Ted. Eva's family is bedrock, but the solidarity was forged
through many years of a difficult marriage.

At the beginning, Eva has often told me, Ted was kind. After
their wedding, Ted and Eva returned to the house of his *padrinos*

in Pharr. Eva was nervous as they sat outside under a tree. "Well, he was beautiful to look at, and I had never been near a man so I was all trembling. I wasn't trembling for love; I was scared. Then he starts touching me, telling me things that I had never, ever heard before. He doesn't tell me he loves me. At the time, I didn't know, but what he wanted was sex. I wasn't ready. But you know he was patient with me. He tells me [about sex] and I say, 'I didn't marry you for that.' And he waits. I thought that was beautiful of him."

Ted finally sent an older woman on the farm, Matiana, to school Eva in matters sexual. "She comes and says she wants to help me fix up the house. I said, 'No, I know how to do that.' So then, how about the cooking? 'No, I know how to cook. I learned from my mom.' So she starts on me and I say, 'Doña Matiana, I didn't marry for that.' He sent everybody on the block to talk to me, and I would just tell them the same thing, 'I didn't marry for that.' They told me that this is what women are for and I told them that I wasn't for that. So there's *la mula* again."

Eva suspected that Ted's family thought she already was pregnant when they married; why else would "such a beautiful man" choose to be with an *india*? They pressured her, but only after two years did Eva became pregnant with Diego. When her parents heard the news from Eva's sister, they overcame their anger and returned to Pharr. Eva suffered from severe morning sickness for the first few months. She didn't understand what had occurred or what was to come. "I thought for months, Joanne, not days but months, how am I going to have this baby? I vomited so much that I thought I'm going to vomit the baby and it's not time. So, I ask my mom, 'I've been wondering, is this why I can't get up, because I'm gonna vomit the baby? Is my mouth big enough?' And she says, 'Where the baby went in, that's where it will come out.' But I didn't see a baby go in." Eva laughs as she delivers this story so many years later, but she sobers at the final line in her mother's explanation. "She didn't give me all the answers, but she just said that Ted had put the baby in me. I had nothing to do with it, see. He did."

Eva was still pregnant when she decided to join her parents and siblings in their move north to Oregon. The family lived close to Nyssa in a labor camp in Parma, Idaho. Ted stayed in Pharr on Mr. Brown's farm to renew his contract as a bracero. He couldn't leave until he had papers for legal residency.

For five years, Eva wrote letters on Ted's behalf. She queried the U.S. president and the governor of Oregon. "I wrote everywhere. I wanted my husband over here." Though Eva had documentation, immigration officials would sometimes raid fields where Eva worked. "They would take me in and make fun of me in the car, saying that they had to get me a husband because I was so young and I shouldn't sleep alone. I would be wet up to my neck because I was so small and the beets were so big. At that time, I was very quiet; now, I would shut them up in no time at all."

One morning as she left the labor camp, Eva's water broke. Diego was born in Nyssa the next day. Four days later, Eva was back picking potatoes. "I look back now and I say, 'It's a miracle that you're alive' because the baby was only four days old and the early potatoes you do at four in the morning. We finished the potatoes but it wasn't good, so Daddy says 'Let's go to Washington because we're not making any money here.' The baby must have been maybe fifteen, twenty days old and we went to Puyallup to pick raspberries and black caps. It rained every day in picking season, so I put my baby in a little box with plastic on him."

A worker like Eva had no choice but to take her children to the fields. In the late 1950s, when Eva's family moved to Nyssa, the average income for migrant workers was between one and two thousand dollars a year.[1] Even workers who were part of the bracero program weren't paid enough for adequate housing, health services, or access to education. The reforms of the 1960s and '70s were still a dream for Latino families.

During a visit with Ted, Eva became pregnant again with her second child, Chayo. She brought both children when she picked onions and beets, leaving them in the car. One day, she heard a man running toward the fields shouting, "Who are the parents of the children in the black car?"

"It was me," Eva acknowledges. "He says, 'Come quick.' So I run back to the car where Diego and Chayo were." She had left the windows slightly open and some finely chopped alfalfa had drifted inside. Diego, who was old enough to sit up, had closed the windows. "By the time I got there, Diego was choking and the baby was full of flies and had maggots in her eyes." Eva feared that the man, Homer Heights, would call children's services and have her kids taken from her. Instead, Heights offered to take her home, talking to Eva en route. "He starts investigating me," Eva says. "I told him why I was working and everything that was happening and he says, 'I will help you.'"

Heights and his wife gave Eva food and some money for the children. More important, they petitioned a friend, Senator Wayne Morse, on behalf of Ted. "Immigration found Ted in the fields in Texas," Eva says, "They handed him the papers right there." Now free to travel, Ted didn't join his family in Nyssa. "I called Mr. Brown and he says, 'He's gone.' He stayed away for three months and I didn't know where he was." Eva shakes her head, as though Ted's actions were a country so foreign she can't imagine traveling

there. "When we got married, people said that either I was pregnant or he just wanted his papers. When he finally got them, he
went to California. He found a job driving a bus; he always loved
driving big rigs. When he couldn't make it in California, he found
a way back here."

The afternoon before our Chinese dinner at Chana and Brown's,
Eva suggested a drive to show me where her first house once
stood. Out Highway 26, a green sign points up the hill to "Nyssa
Heights." We climbed past the Nyssa graveyard to a patchwork of
well-irrigated wheat, bean, and cornfields punctuated by an occasional farmhouse. From the summit, Eva read the landscape like a
storybook of her years in the fields, often pregnant, ill, or hungry.
"*Mira*," she pointed toward one of the bright blue portable toilets
on the roadside. "We never had those." Then she nodded toward
the steep hill. "I used to push my kids to the doctors in a wheelbar-
row." One experience surfaced that opened the floodgates to others. Before Chayo was born, Eva was picking beans one day when
she began to bleed. "I walked with Diego in my arms to tell Ted.
He said, 'Go home.' He could have said 'Hop on the tractor, I'll
take you back.' No, he let me walk. And he never came."

Eva jumped ahead in the story. A few years later, Eva and Ted
journeyed to Guadalajara to see his family. Eva stayed in Mexico
when Ted returned to California to work. Ted's family had ini-
tially welcomed Eva, but she always suspected they considered
her beneath Ted. After his departure, they locked her in the house
when they went out. Determined to escape, she called Ted. His
employer sent her money to come to California. She arrived bleeding from another pregnancy. "One day, he gets up to leave for
work and I started having all these pains. The kids were saying,

'What's the matter, mommy?' My stomach hurts. Pretty soon, I felt this thing come out. I looked in there and it was a baby." Within the same day, Eva discovered she was carrying twins when she miscarried again. "I started having those pains again, I started to sweat. I felt this other thing, something on my leg that moved. I didn't want to see, but I knew I had to. I think it was the umbilical cord."

When Ted returned that evening, he said nothing to Eva's story of the miscarriage. "He starts making a place to go to bed. Two days go by and I couldn't get up. Now, I know I must have been out of my mind because I took those babies and I tried to flush them down the toilet. I flushed and flushed and they never left. Wrap 'em up and take 'em out of there, I told myself. But I saw their little faces and hair and feet and then I knew what I was going to do. Dig. So I did. I found a place where it was soft and put them in there. And as I did, I was thinking this is wrong, wrong, wrong. But who was there to tell?"

All felt still, the air thick with humidity as she parked the car at the edge of road. Eva pointed to a thick stand of clover that marks a milestone: the family's first rented house and private space. After their move from Texas, Eva and the kids lived with her parents, even when Ted joined them. "It was really hard. My sister was already married and my little brothers had the living room. Ted and I and our kids were in the bathroom. That was our room, a tiny four-by-something bathroom; we had to cover the bathtub and make it our bed. We had no food. Ted didn't have a job." When they found their own place, Eva thought life would improve.

One day, Eva left with the kids to visit her friend Lucinda. Ted argued against it, saying that he didn't want the children in the sun. Later, Lucinda revealed that Ted had propositioned her. Eva endured Ted's infidelity and neglect through her next pregnancy. "Ralph was born premature because I was out in the fields; there were weeds this big and you had to pull them by the roots. I just started bleeding and nobody could find Ted."

By the time she was pregnant with Maria, Eva laid down the law. Ted was "running around with a lot of women then." One in particular, Suzy, lived nearby in an area called "the reservation" for its population of Indians from New Mexico. When Eva was about to deliver, Suzy knocked on the door one night. Ted rose to depart. Eva said, "If you go, don't come back." He left. Eva piled the kids into a wagon to go to her mother's in case her water broke. But Ted surprised her that night and returned. He drove her to the hospital, brought the baby home, and helped find the *padrinos* and plan the baptismal party. But Eva had made up her mind. "I told him on the way to the hospital, 'When I have my baby and you bring me home, I do not want to see you anymore. I do not want you in the house.' He didn't listen. The last guest left the [baptismal] party. I had already packed his bags. I gave him the car keys, I put his things outside, and I locked the door." Eva stuck to her ultimatum. "I had nothing. I didn't have a job. But I knew how to crochet so I crocheted a whole bunch of covered bottles with little heads that looked like puppies. I pedaled them to the stores and I bought my babies' milk with that. I stuck it out. Ted would send us money and I would put it in an envelope and send it back."

Ted was gone for six or seven months. That winter turned bitter cold. Every night Eva's father would knock three times on her window. "I would say, 'Daddy, I'm fine,' and he would go to bed. One night, I remember it was so cold and I had no kerosene for heat. So I put all the kids on the bed, with every inch of clothing we had for heat. Then there's a knock at the door. I didn't want to

get up but I did. When I opened the little curtain, Ted was standing there. I wanted to cry, I wanted to laugh, I wanted to hug him,
I wanted to kick him—everything together. But I said, 'What do
you want?' He was really sad and skinny and awful looking and
he says, 'I want to come in.' I say, 'Here? Uh-uh, go further on
down the road.' I let the curtain fall. He knew I wasn't going to
open the door.

"*La mula*. So he goes to my dad and my dad comes and knocks
on the window. 'Genoveva? Open the door.' I say, 'I'll open the
door because you're here. I don't want you to be cold, but I will
not open the door for him.' I opened the door. They both come in
and my dad starts saying, 'This is the way life is. All men do that
[infidelity].' 'Ooh, ' I said, 'You, too? Get out of my house right
now, both of you.'

"And I kicked them out."

Eva says now that she felt certain that her father had not, in
fact, been unfaithful. "But he was talking 'men.'" The show of
solidarity infuriated Eva, but two or three weeks later her father
talked her into taking Ted back in. She relented, but delivered an
ultimatum: home by twelve and help with the kids. "He stayed,"
she says. "He didn't help me, but he didn't go out."

Not that winter, perhaps, but the stories spill out: other sea-
sons, other women. Eva recounts an encounter Chana had in the
local supermarket. A young girl she'd never seen before came up
to her to say, "I'm a Castellanoz, too."

"I couldn't make saliva," Chana recalled of her temporary
paralysis.

Eva recalls another story: On Ted's yearly trips to Mexico, he
brought back photos. One lovely young woman Ted claimed was
his cousin landed on the Castellanoz mantel. Eva, always eager

to extend the boundaries of family, bought a special frame for it. At the time, she worked for Oregon State University as a county extension agent. "Destiny has her way," she says, describing how an unfamiliar name turned up on her list of home visits. At the house, Eva spotted a photo of Ted's cousin in the woman's living room. "I say, 'Oh, I have a photo just like this one.' This woman says, 'Yes, that's your husband's daughter.' I said, 'What?' She answers 'Yeah, they write to him all the time. Here's three letters he hasn't come to pick up.'

"Out of the blue, right into my heart. All those years, he said no, no, no, no. And behind my back . . . "

During dinner, Eva and her family tell stories as we empty paper containers of fried rice and chow mein. Chana describes her family's years in California, where she and Brown ran a store. They had arranged to slowly buy the business when it was abruptly pulled out from under them. They faced racism and, ultimately, huge financial loss. They, like Eva, had to postpone their dream of a house and an economic foundation.

Eva aches when her children suffer—the divorces, the illnesses, the gaps between their dreams and what life delivers. As we carry the dishes to the kitchen, Eva looks toward Chana, who strokes her daughter Lola's waist-length black hair. "My children have suffered a lot," Eva says. "It was sad but I don't look at it in a negative way, because they know how it is. Now I see their kids and they're wonderful parents because of all that they've been through." Chana and Brown didn't let their devastating loss strain the marriage; if anything, says Eva, they are stronger. When they returned to Nyssa, Brown found work in nearby Idaho and Chana at the bank in Ontario. They blended back into the clan, embraced and celebrated.

Eva wishes for each of her children what she doesn't have—a long, stable, and fulfilling marriage. I don't know where Ted is now; I don't ask. Eva still probes for his good qualities: his even temper, his hard-working nature. But for all the searching, the facts remain. "I still don't have the husband that my kids needed. I wanted it like my blouse. I wanted it to fit. My husband was too big; I wanted to cut him to size. He doesn't let me, but that's what I want."

Eva describes the advice she received before her wedding. "It was told to me when I married that this is my cross and I have to carry it." Many Mexican women of Eva's generation grew up with this view of marriage. But even women who accept their lot and end up with a spouse they did not choose are not without power; many find meaning in their children, their *comadres*, and their communities. Eva, however, goes beyond acceptance to rebel against carrying the cross. "Heck! Then what do I have you for? Let's both carry it. And whatever you do to me, you do to Jesus Christ. This is what binds you together. You should be able to come home and help me cook, be partners, not slaves. Partners in marriage, partners in work, partners in bed, partners in parenting." Despite her frustration, Eva says, "My husband cannot give me all of happiness; it starts with me. I need a partner like a door needs a hinge, but it's still a door, and even without the hinge, it still can close."

Leaving Chana and Brown's, I imprint the image of Ted and Eva hanging above the mantel. Years later, I will discover that this is not a photo of just-married young people. A photographer spliced the two pictures together in the 1990s. Given the course of Eva's life, the artificial placement seems ironic but fitting. Yet, even after I know about this alteration, I'm haunted by Eva's young eyes. They have not yet taken in the enormity of what is to come: the deaths, the ongoing despair of life with and without Ted, her own illness and those of so many others who will come to her. She doesn't yet realize that she, like her mother, will become a healer. Yet, the eyes look out with an openness that embraces the not-yet-known, the pleasure and sorrow that will join hands at every juncture.

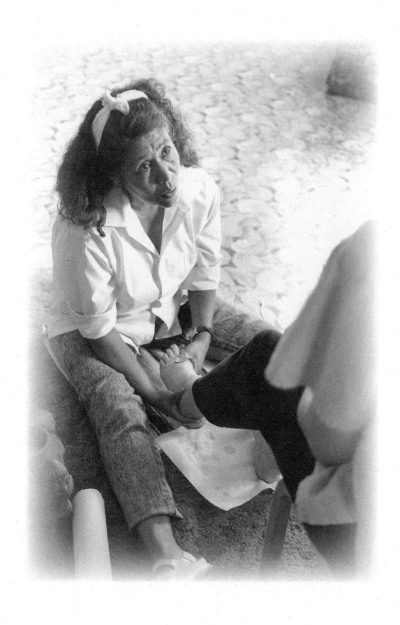

PART II

Healing

If you want to call me anything, call me a wounded healer. I had to have death so that I could understand. I had to be wounded before I could try to heal.

—EVA CASTELLANOZ

9

The Call

La Enfermedad: The doctor said, "Something
terrible has happened." They hooked me up
to machines and, you know, at that time, I
didn't even talk. I was just there quiet.

El Remedio: He [God] called to me and like the *mula*
that I am, I said "No!" He looked straight into my
eyes with all that beautiful love and said, "From this
day forward, your life is not going to be your own."

ON A HOT SUMMER DAY IN 1968, Eva was working the fields
with her sister Gorda and all of their children. Nine months pregnant, she bent over her rounded belly to pick cherries. All at once,
Maria Elena, Gorda's daughter, grew listless, then feverish. Eva
knew something was wrong. "Growing up around my mom, we
knew about fevers," she says. They headed to the doctor's office
with the children. He examined Maria Elena and found nothing
serious. He sent the families on their way with some medication.

By eleven o'clock the next morning, Maria Elena was dead. The other children sickened quickly.

"They would just fall down, " Eva remembers. "They would be playing, and then black stuff would be oozing out of them." Eva and Gorda rushed the entire group to the hospital. Contaminated cherries, the doctors surmised, could have been the source. "They said they had never seen that disease," Eva recalls. "To date, I do not remember what it was. Maybe I chose not to know." The hospital quarantined the sick children. "We had nine at that time in the hospital—my sister's children and five of mine," Eva says. "I stayed with them because my sister was mentally deranged by her child's death." Two of Eva's family, Maria and Marty, worsened; the doctors feared they might not survive the first night. "Five of mine so sick," Eva repeats.

Five children sick, several close to death. This story carries a tragic echo of long ago in Valle de Santiago, of Eva's parents walking the streets with sick and dying children, when her mother's knowledge of healing was exhausted. *Just by saying it. You lose your mind; you don't remember. It's like a fairy tale. It's not real, but to us, it's real.* The *testimonios* of poor families, the many children lost. The story too big to tell.

But Eva's story would have a different ending. Maria and Marty stabilized; the others recovered. Eva finally went home to attend to chores that had piled up. When she walked in, her labor pains started. She drove herself back to the hospital. The same doctor who had just treated the children now checked her contractions. Eva recalls that his face "went white" as he wheeled her to the delivery room.

"The doctor said, 'Something terrible has happened.' They hooked me up to machines and you know, that time of my life, I didn't even talk. I was just there quiet. I think he was getting nervous because he hollered at me and asked who had come with me. I said nobody. 'Where's your husband?' I didn't know where he was. The doctor brought papers for me to sign because he had to go into me to save the baby or me. By this time, he thought the baby was dead and I might not make it. Those were his words."

"Somebody put a mask on my face and said for me to count back from one hundred. I started counting and I don't know when I started seeing—aah!—all my life. A lot of things I didn't even know, places I didn't remember. They just started coming on like a movie. I know now that eternity has no time and it has no limits and it has no bounds and it's all light and it's beautiful. In what seems like no time at all, that was over with and I started floating on a beautiful road of light. No pain, no thoughts, no nothing. Just beautiful. I started seeing people that knew me and that I knew. They spoke to me but not with their mouths. They spoke with their minds. They had hats of light. They were very happy. I started seeing colors and everything around me sang in different tunes or melodies. Finally, I come to these doors that open to the outside. The Lord was on a cloud on the other side. There were lots of singing children with wings. He stretched his arms out to me. When I started approaching, I could feel him loving me with some love that I had never felt before. Just out of him onto me, not just over me, but into and through me. Not with his mouth but with his mind, he says, 'Come,' and he stretched out his arms. He called to me and like the *mula* that I am, I stopped short and quick—I can remember that—and said 'No!' I started thinking and arguing. I told him, 'What are my kids going to do? I can't come because they are just barely out of the hospital.' And don't think that I was just talking—like the true *mula* that I am, I was mad! I cussed at him. Then, I remembered my baby. I said, 'How about that baby I carried for nine months? You cannot have him'—I knew it was a boy—'He's mine.' I said all these awful words. But he loved me anyway. He's not like us that we do a little thing to each other and I don't love you anymore. No, he loved me more. He kept stretching his arms out to me and I said, 'No.'

"It was just beautiful, indescribable. There are no words, none, that can describe him. He stretched out his arms again and again, and I said no. He says, 'Okay. You're going back.' He looked straight into my eyes with all that beautiful love and said, 'From this day forward, your life is not going to be your own.' I said, 'To hell with you. What I want is to go back.'

"Ten days later, I woke with a priest by my side. I wanted to talk but I couldn't. The nurse comes in and says, 'Do you want to see the baby?' I didn't remember. I said, 'Ooh, you mean they have him, dead?' I thought he had died. But she says, 'He's beautiful. He's got lots of dark hair just like you.'"

Eva went home with her ninth child, Cami. "For a long time, I thought I was on a cloud. I was so happy. Everything was beautiful. I knew things; I was scared because I knew things that were going to happen. I knew your name before I ever saw you. From that day forward, too, I just found people at my door. People knew—or God knew—it was time for healing, and he let people know in their hearts."

Some stories demand to be told and retold. If you have been healed when others said you were beyond hope, if you have emerged from an experience you cannot explain, if you have groped for language to convey the fullness of an event but found yourself perched at its edge, then you know such stories. They inhabit the core of your being. You invite listeners over a narrative bridge; they may cross or not.

Eva told me this story when we met in 1989, sitting in her backyard as the hummingbird fluttered overhead. She has repeated it many times in our taped interviews and in public settings. I've read versions told to a fellow writer and folklorist from Idaho, Bob McCarl. The story tells of change on many levels: Eva's deliverance from the edge of death; retreat from the near loss of five children that would have paralleled her mother's experience; the shift from being "just quiet" to speaking up, and from individual suffering to alleviating the pain of others. It is a story unique to Eva and one common to healers cross-culturally who tell of being "called" to their gift after a period of hardship.[1] In *The Gift*, writer Lewis Hyde characterizes a gift as something we do not get by our own efforts, that we labor to develop, and that we must pass on. Though Hyde does not deal specifically with healing, the description is apt. Many people have the potential to be healers, but few follow the path. What guides them to healing is the combination of something outside of them—the call—and their willingness to labor in the service of the gift or *don*.[2]

Most healers experience their call as life altering. Elizabeth de la Portilla details this pattern among *curanderas* and *curanderos* in San Antonio, Texas.[3] Each received the gift in a spiritual fashion and then transformed his or her life. Only after such a conversion can the healer help others change their lives. The community must acknowledge this metamorphosis; it cannot happen in isolation.

Today, many *curanderas* in the United States and Mexico are undergoing another more collective transformation: reclaiming their roots as *indias*. In tracing *curanderismo*'s history, many scholars traditionally highlighted the European contributions. When the Spanish colonized Mexico in the sixteenth century, they carried with them a patchwork of healing methods. Hispano-Arabic medicine included the Greek idea of humors (blood, phlegm, black and yellow bile), revived in the Spanish renaissance, and the Arabic concept of health as a balance—within the body and between an individual and the environment. Judeo-Christian beliefs permeate *curanderismo*; many prayers and practices have biblical roots. Healers often point to a passage from Corinthians that affirms their status as vessels: "One man, through the spirit, has the gift of wise speech . . . another, gifts of healing."[4] The cross and the triangle of the Holy Trinity are central symbols in ritual practices.

Now, younger scholars, especially Latinos and feminists, look to the indigenous belief systems and practices that predated and mixed with European imports. The Spanish recorded an extensive repertoire of herbs used by indigenous peoples. This knowledge still informs Eva's work. She combs the land around Nyssa and travels to Mexico for the herbs she needs. Other dimensions of traditional healing were passed down through oral tradition. Near the Texas border where Eva's family lived, Native American tribes contributed rituals and practices that merged with the ever-evolving system of healing. For example, some contemporary *curanderas* in south Texas use sweetgrass for smudging ceremonies.[5] *Curanderismo* is fluid, an improvisational mix of borrowed and blended elements. It's difficult to tease out what came from European Catholicism, what from indigenous groups in Mexico and the southwestern United States. Some aspects of *curanderismo* echo African healing practices that slaves brought to the New World between the 1500s and the 1800s. Both stress relationships with ancestors and look to the earth as a place of healing.[6]

Healers are part of a larger group of Mexicans and Mexican Americans now regenerating an Indian past. In *México Profundo: Reclaiming a Civilization*, Guillermo Bonfil Batalla underscores the Indian foundation of a "new Mexico," one he contrasts with the western "Imaginary Mexico" born of colonization. Batalla details the ongoing strength of Mesoamerican civilization: the foundation of agriculture, the balance of human beings with the natural world, the dedication of each individual to a larger community. Many view contemporary Mexico's *mestizaje* as a blending of European and indigenous cultures. In contrast, Batalla argues that these cultures were not synthesized; the indigenous was "de-Indianized."[7]

Many Mexican and Mexican American testimonios, both oral and written, reveal similar themes of resistance to colonization and the resilience of Mesoamerican culture.[8] To critics who see cultural renewal as romantic, Edén Torres responds, "Reclaiming a mythic past rooted in concepts of indigenous America—whether or not it is romanticized—is part of the group's movement toward self-definition and away from victimization and devaluation."[9] In Torres's view, such a move is a healing response to centuries of collective trauma.

Curanderas such as Eva, suspicious of the "dress that doesn't fit," may use the symbols and teachings of Catholicism but emphasize their Indian heritage. Eva also recounts tense encounters between Church teachings and indigenous beliefs. Immediately after she returned from the hospital with Cami, Eva went to see the priest at St. Briget's. She described being "called," how she had died, and how she had begun to "see" and know things before they were evident to others. The priest said, "What are you talking about? That's from the devil. Put an end to that and don't think about such things."

Transformations in individual lives often become stories. Stories then shape lives. We become what we tell, affirming the metamorphosis with every retelling. Each time Eva relates the story of being called, she attests to coming to power as a *curandera*. Each time, she embodies the paradox of the gift: the more an individual gives to her community, the more abundant her resources grow. Each time, she testifies to the spirit of *la mula* in the quiet girl maturing into the woman who speaks out. Undaunted by that grandest of interlocutors, Eva talked back. She could do so, she says now, because love made her unafraid. "I tell you about the love of God," Eva says, "but not God, God, God of religion, religion, religion. He didn't talk to me. He just covered me with his eyes. Nobody can take it away from me, because I saw it. And I'm going to use it."

10

Magical Thinking

La Enfermedad: Often, she [Eva's mother] didn't
have time to do this or gather that. She would
say, "Go get me some bark from the mesquite."
And I would. By that time, I knew that this was
not right for the ailment of that person. "Mama,
you shouldn't have given her that mesquite
bark because that was not her problem."

El Remedio: She said, "*Mija*, I didn't have anything
else. God will give me the strength. God will give
me the way." And, by faith, they would be healed.

TWO YOUNG MEN LINGER in the driveway of Eva's house
on a June day in 1999. People waiting to be healed—a scene I've
witnessed many times over the decade I've known Eva. The men,
handsome young Mexicans, came from a migrant camp in Idaho.
One man's jeans bag at the crotch; his baseball cap completes the
urban look. The other, unsmiling under a thick mustache, sports

tighter jeans and a broad-brimmed cowboy hat. Like many of Eva's clients, they have no appointment and know about her work through word-of-mouth. Luis, the man in the baseball cap, has been here before, returning now with his troubled friend, Jorge.

Luis urges Jorge forward. "*Mucho gusto*," Eva grasps his hand as they are introduced. "*Tengo un problema*," he starts to speak, then waves a hand in the air, as if the problems are too many to enumerate. He seems so agitated that I worry I may be a distraction, but Eva motions for me to stay. We follow the walkway past the miniature koi pond to the casita. Inside, Luis speaks for the frustrated Jorge. He has problems in love, with friends, and at his job. He fights with the other workers; he can't sleep or eat. Eva nods, for she sees the multiple *niveles*, all the levels at once: physical, mental, spiritual, and emotional.

Curanderas do not separate body from mind or spirit; they seek balance among all and between individuals and families or communities. Eva recalls the people who came to her mother, Conchita. "Often, she didn't have time to do this or gather that. She would say, 'Go get me some bark from the mesquite.' And I would. By that time, I knew that this was not right for the ailment of that person. 'Mama, you shouldn't have given her that mesquite bark because that was not her problem.' She said, '*Mija* [my daughter, from *mi hija*], I didn't have anything else.' And by faith, they would be healed." Eva learned from watching her mother; she also developed her own style through years of practice. *Curanderas* are flexible and creative, making use of whatever is at hand.

Eva drops to her knees to massage both men's feet with oil. "I like to touch people a lot. The first thing I do if I'm going to massage any part of your body is to make a triangle—Padre, Hijo, Espíritu Santo—Father, Son, and Holy Spirit. Everything is up, not down. Because we are already down by not having a job, by whatever is hurting us." The feet are critical. "Everything about your body is right in your feet." Eva gently questions Jorge. Does he have family here? No, his mother and brothers live in a village near Oaxaca; his mother has been ill. A girlfriend? Jorge smiles. Not yet but he has hopes. A healer, Eva says, must consider the web of work, family, friends, religion, and community. Illness may spring from natural or supernatural causes. One of the *curandera*'s tasks is to tease out the source. "Every illness has its story," writes *curandera* Elena Avila, "and the job of the healer is to uncover that story."[1]

As Jorge grows comfortable, he reveals details to Eva. He awakes terrified at night. He may be suffering from *susto* (fright), often described as "soul loss." Extreme fear can prompt this illness, but so can overwhelming demands on a person. Some scholars of cross-cultural medicine argue that *susto* allows adults to flee social life at times of great stress.[2] Healers such as Elena Avila, describe *susto* as a rupture of the most vulnerable part of the self, the spiritual aura. Avila is also a psychiatric nurse who frequently treats rape victims; she believes their souls flee their violated auras. The *curandera* must "call back" the person.

Eva describes her process: "My mama used to say, if you get scared, your spirit stays behind. We have to do a ritual of speaking the word: we think it, then we speak it, then we do it. My mother had her own prayers, but I use the ninety-first psalm, the specialist for healing *susto*." The psalm solicits protection through the words, "There shall no evil befall thee, neither shall any plague come nigh thy dwelling/For he shall give his angels charge over thee, to keep thee in all thy ways." To the Catholic symbolism Eva adds the Native elements of using "incense with little stones;

you bring together the harmony of the four corners of the earth. Call the name, like 'Joanne.' '*Me voy*'—I'm coming. I call you and you answer, that's how your spirit comes back." *Susto*, Eva says, permeates a house. "There's a feeling when you enter a house and know that something is not right."

Susto, *mal de ojo*, *mal aire*, and other illnesses are sometimes called "culture bound syndromes."[3] Our bodies house pain, but our cultures shape suffering. Some illnesses don't translate into other cultural frameworks. When a Mexican American experiences a loss of spirit or a similar illness, *el remedio* must culturally match *la enfermedad*. Healers act as cultural and linguistic translators. Calling *mal de ojo* the "evil eye," the most common English rendering, implies a malice that may not exist. A better translation, argues Avila, is "illness caused by staring," especially at young children, who are most often afflicted by *mal de ojo*. Many cultures protect infants from a stranger's gaze with talismans: the *hamesh* in Jewish tradition, which resembles a hand, and the *figa* in Italy, among others. Each guards a child against being unsettled by too much attention or envy.

Mal do ojo differs from *mal puesto*—a hex or a curse. *Curanderismo* encompasses indigenous beliefs in negative spirits as well as elements of European witchcraft. While *curanderas* appeal to supernatural powers to heal, *brujas* (witches) harness those forces for harm.[4] Eva believes that *brujas* exist. She describes a man who was certain he'd been cursed. After two weeks in a Portland medical center, his leg continued to atrophy. When his other leg manifested the same symptoms, he came to Eva. "I prayed for him and he started healing." Eva sometimes has to defend herself against charges of *brujería*. But the true *brujas*, Eva says, are the so-called healers who charge exorbitant sums. "I see people," she says, "how they believe and my heart cries because they're used by others because of their innocent faith."

Terms such as *susto* and *mal de ojo* entered academe in the United States during the mid-twentieth century. Between 1965 and 1976, new waves of Mexicans crossed the border for work. In response, the government mandated studies of Mexican health-care beliefs and techniques. Early research cataloged folk practices like Eva's but often without cultural context. Many studies overemphasized *susto* and distinctly cultural illnesses; focus on "exotic" diseases may have kept researchers from considering *curanderismo* as a medical system with its own integrity.[5] A second group of studies went beyond cataloging to interpretation. When the interpreters used Freudian and other Western lenses, distortion resulted. Some call *curanderismo* "folk psychiatry." In fact, Eva does treat problems that Western doctors would label "psychological"; this distinction, however, suggests a divide between mind and body not relevant to Mexican American healing. Some researchers have also critiqued *curanderas* as essentially conservative, maintaining the status quo by reintegrating the sick person into a sexist and unfair society.[6] But *curanderas* seek rebalance on multiple levels. Eva does "call back" a *susto* sufferer to be enfolded into a community. At the same time, she works tirelessly to forge a society marked by equality for women and immigrants. Healing happens in social as well as individual bodies.

I watch Eva's strong fingers knead the flesh of Jorge's feet. Massage is her entry point. Some healers, called *sobadores*, focus on massage; *yerberos* specialize in herbs, *parteras* in midwifery, *señoras* in reading cards (Tarot or standard decks), and *espiritualistas* in caring for spiritual needs. Eva practices all aspects of *curanderismo* because "I'm the only one around here." Her knowledge of herbs in extensive. She also reads cards, using a regular deck rather than Tarot. "I don't guess and I don't divine," Eva says. "I read the symbols." Her mother didn't use cards often. "She was very Catholic," Eva explains. Conchita considered card reading "pagan," but it was precisely this indigenous, precolonial heritage that called to Eva as a child. When the family lived in Reynosa, her mother would go off to buy and sell goods. Eva would go to the cantina where a "gypsy woman" read cards. Below the entrance rested a stone step where Eva would hover, listening and watching. "I loved it, and I wanted to learn," she says. "So I carried it inside of me." Above all, Eva identifies with the spiritual aspect of healing, reckoning with good and evil, attending to "things we cannot see" to make intelligible a larger universe.

Eva points to a chart of the body with a line running through the center. "*Mira*," she indicates invisible energy fields. Jorge's aura, Eva has determined from his story, pushes people away. *Susto* may be the problem, but in any case, the first step is a *limpia*—a cleansing or "sweeping" to remove negative forces. Jorge nods, accepting her suggestion. If he had disagreed, Eva might have reconsidered her diagnosis. *Curanderas* share power. "I don't say, 'I'm going to find out what's wrong,'" Eva explains. "I say, 'Let's find out together.'" Clients determine the session's length. "I don't set a timer. I wait until they are ready." Today is Saturday, and the traditional times for *limpias* are Wednesday, Friday, and Sunday. Eva asks Jorge to return the next day. Until then, he will carry a protective medallion. As the men saunter to their truck, Jorge fingers the amulet.

The power of words, charms, and religious icons remains central to Mexican and Mexican American culture. Detractors thus dismiss *curanderismo* as backward and dangerous—as "magical thinking." But most medical practitioners admit to the complexity of healing. Curing—ridding the body of pathogens—is often contrasted with healing—a broad process with social and psychological dimensions. Doctors cannot always delineate the boundaries. All medicine works on two levels: symbolic and physical. Healing happens in the connective tissue between language, beliefs and rituals, and physiological processes. In asking whether a practice "works," we need to consider our measuring tools.[7] Western medicine, so adept at erasing disease symptoms, may fail at healing, at the "making whole" that harnesses belief and restores equilibrium. A person may retain physical symptoms, yet be healed—balanced, at peace, able to manage sickness, even ready to face death. The chronic illnesses that plague modern postindustrial nations like the United States are particularly resistant to the straightforward cures that work for infectious diseases.

Furthermore, the division between Western medicine's curing and the holism of healing is not as complete as it seems. In *The Cure Within: A History of Mind-Body Medicine*, Anne Harrington follows Mesmer's power of suggestion to Norman Cousin's healing through laughter to contemporary New Age thought. She points to our yearning for the old-style doctor who took a pastoral interest in our well-being. Beyond the narrative of "tissue, blood, and biochemistry," all of us want stories of human beings and the meaning of suffering.[8] When we face illness and ultimately death, we crave from medical doctors the comfort that people have always sought from healers. Journalist David Rieff writes of his mother, Susan Sontag, that although "she had no time for so-called alternative medicine . . . when all was said and done, my mother's relationship with her principal doctor can only be fully understood—and was only fully effective—because it was in some ways as shamanistic as the relations our ancestors knew before the advent of modern medicine."[9]

Until the European Enlightenment, this healing was women's work. When men wrested that power to create institutional medicine, magic and science parted ways, then grew opposed. The empirical world of the observable trumped the supernatural world of faith. But scholars of *curanderismo* argue that in a *curandera*'s world, magic is empirical. Its reality is social rather than scientific. "It deals with objects and observable events; it is based upon a systematic body of knowledge; it has evolved . . . and it produces results that can be both directly and indirectly perceived, recorded and tested."[10] To understand how *curanderismo* works, we must suspend Western assumptions about the unseen, about the divisions of mind, body, and spirit, about what it means to heal.

Jorge and Luis return the next afternoon. Jorge's dark-rimmed eyes and disheveled hair make him look as though he spent the night in the Nyssa Tavern. Eva welcomes the two men to the casita. She gathers the ritual objects for the *limpia*: bunches of herbs, a pan for the mesquite coals, and a long piece of light-purple cloth. *Curanderas* use everyday objects such as eggs, lemons, and onions to protect the patient and to absorb the negative forces "swept" from the aura. "I am a symbol person who learns that way," Eva says. The sheer purple fabric has multiple associations: royalty, Christ the King, the drape fabric on Catholic altars during Semana Santa (Easter week). "It means new beginnings, resurrection."

Some of Eva's other *remedios* rely on imitative or sympathetic magic, practices in which a symbol produces its likeness in effecting a cure.[11] If Jorge had come with the heaviness of a broken heart, Eva would have given him a small, blue cloth heart with a zigzag line cut through the center. She once gave me a similar heart after a disastrous romance, advising me to "take one small stitch each day and you will find your way." Sometimes, Eva walks the troubled person to the window of the casita. "Drink cups of sunshine. It starts with bringing sun into your heart," she says. "My parents did that for healing. They'd take a *jarrito*, a little Mexican cup, and hold it up to the early sun and drink." I've seen Eva offer depressed clients *mejorana* (marjoram). "In Spanish, it means 'better.' So I don't just use the herb, I tell the meaning. 'Listen to its name. Drink a cup when you rise in the morning. Boil the rest in a half-gallon of water. Put it in your mop, in a squirt bottle, squirt all around your house, outside and in. See if things don't get better.'"

Eva acknowledges the limitations of symbols and the power of scientific medicine. *Curanderismo* has changed with technological advances. *Hueseros*, traditional bonesetters, disappeared when confronted with the superior methods of Western doctors. If she suspected Jorge's problem required a doctor, she would call the emergency room at nearby Ontario's Holy Rosary Medical Center. If Luis could not drive him, Eva would call a cab and pay for it. Many immigrants, especially those recently arrived, go to *curanderas* for financial as well as cultural reasons. "My people don't have much money," Eva says. "They work very hard in the onions. I wish one of those doctors would go out there from six thirty in the morning to five thirty in the afternoon. Then he would know how it is for my people."

While Eva is called on to heal multiple forms of illness, most often she encounters "wounds of the spirit" that require *limpias*. Standing next to Jorge, she holds a set of yellowed, water-stained pages—her mother's *limpia* prayer inscribed many years before.

Eva explains, "I sweep them and I pray; I have a lot of beautiful, powerful prayers. I say, 'Let all enemies melt like a candle would melt by the fire or by the sun.'" She beckons Jorge into the next room behind a curtain for privacy. I hear her begin, "We're asking the Lord Jesus to give you his grace so that nothing that your enemies want to do against you will prevail. We're asking our creator to give you a little humbleness in your life . . . "

I cannot see them but I imagine the scene. Eva performed a *limpia* for me at a dark time in my life. She directed me to the same room where the young man now rests. In a tall chair that made me feel childlike and open, my back faced west to turn away from my old life. Mesquite coals burned in a pan under my feet. Smoke swirled up around my shoulders. Eva circled me, reciting the *limpia* prayer in Spanish, "sweeping" the front, back, and sides of my body with smoke from the burning sage. Another cleansing followed. I squinted one eye open to see a crucifix with candles affixed to either side. Holy water dripped onto my hands and feet. Eva draped the sweet-smelling purple cloth lightly over my head. After each prayer, I added "so be it" to Eva's recitations. Her words lulled me into a trancelike state. I left feeling light, deeply renewed, indeed cleansed.

Why had the *limpia* had that effect? Did I believe because Eva believes? Did the incense and human touch and familiar Catholic symbols offer comfort? The left hemisphere of the brain decodes most linguistic symbols—a rational, linear process. But the right hemisphere interprets the condensed meaning of ritual symbols in a more holistic way. We experience their force emotionally, often without our conscious awareness.[12]

Jorge seems tranquil as he emerges from the next room. He removes a few bills from his wallet, which Eva gratefully accepts.

Curanderas do not charge; healing is a gift—from God to the healer, from the healer to the sick person, who then gives back as he or she can. People offer money, chickens, clothing, buckets of fruit, a few onions, or household goods such as lamps. "I have so many lamps!" Eva laughs. "But what they bring, that's not important. It comes back." As Jorge gets ready to leave, he smiles, the first time I have seen his face relax.

———

In the years since I watched Eva help Jorge, I've wondered about his life. Did he return to see his sick mother in Oaxaca? Did he find love here? Based on Eva's stories and the many people I've seen her heal, I imagine Jorge's path. My musings might fit his life or the lives of others. They are fictive *testimonios*.

Here's one possibility: Jorge meets a young woman in the onion fields. Call her Dolores. Imagine her oval face and almond eyes. Maybe she dreams of finding work at the Oreida potato processing plant and buying a house; perhaps she yearns to return to Mexico, and the family she left behind. Jorge and Dolores work side by side; at night, they attend English classes at the community college. When they marry, they return to Eva for a wedding *lazo*—the symbol of their lifelong connection. They have a daughter and name her Gracia, for the thanks they offer as their lives improve. Surely they invite Eva to the baptism ceremony at their rented house—small but brimming with flowers and tables heavy with roasted pig, tamales, tortillas, and salsa. But more difficult days await beyond the celebration. When Gracia grows ill, the family cannot afford a doctor. The story they tell upon returning to Eva's casita is one she has heard many times: undiagnosed illness, financial struggles, despair settled into body and soul. Their world is out of balance—individuals with their spirits, a family with the larger world. It is a story like all the others; it is a tale unique to Jorge and his family. This is how Eva sees it, for each person who comes to her is "the God I wait for."

Maybe Jorge and Dolores leave the fields for other work, as Eva's children have. One of them could find a job in Boise that offers health insurance for the family. Will they then circle back to Eva's? Jorge and Dolores might follow the path of many Mexican Americans, alternating and using both systems. *Curanderismo* emerged from complex cultural collisions. Today, another set of encounters is reshaping a *curandera*'s work. A hybridized third way is evolving, an integration of Mexican healing, Western medicine, and other traditions. Certain elements will remain constant: the balance of mind, body, spirit, and emotion; the need for community recognition of a healer. But new technologies and social shifts are creating a *mezcla* (a mix) writes Elizabeth de la Portilla. She describes one young Latina who studies Buddhism and meditates each morning, practices that will make their way into her healing work.[13]

I don't know what the future holds for Jorge. But I feel certain that if his mother in Oaxaca dies while he is in the United States, he will find his way to Eva's, for his brothers will mourn in Mexico and he will mourn in Idaho, the holes in his heart gaping. Western medicine is strong—wounds can be stitched and pills can be prescribed for pain. But the death of a loved one lances the heart in different ways. A doctor opens one door, but a *curandera* unlocks the passage through which Jorge might walk toward wholeness. In Eva's casita, he can sit beneath a purple cloth as prayers in Spanish shower down on him, and he remembers who he is and where he came from and even who he might become. Surely there is magic in that.

II

Drinking in the Pain

La Enfermedad: Toe was not just my son. He was
my beautiful friend. How could I have been able to
take his death, to see those eyes close forever?

El Remedio: God knew I wasn't going to be
able to handle Toe's death. He knew it and he
anaesthetized me so I could drink in the pain
little by little, not *swoosh!* all at one time.

EARLY EVENING LIGHT SATURATES THE MINT FIELDS on
the road out of Nyssa. As we drive up to the cemetery, the temperature drops five degrees below the steamy 106 at Eva's house. On
the hillside, mausoleums alternate with floral displays that spell
out "Dad" and "Beloved." Elaborately carved headstones rest next
to simple granite slabs. Our destination is a four-by-six rectangle
of pinkish marble that Eva made a special trip to Mexico to pur-
chase. From near the base of the stone, Eva yanks out a plastic bag.
Inside, pieces of weathered notebook paper curl at the edges. We

perch on adjacent grave markers, the granite cool beneath us. Eva reads, "Dear Toe, We miss you very much. Love Lolo." "Dear Toe, We are thinking about you. Love, Sergio Picasso."

Since 1989, Eva's stories have kept alive the spirit of her eighth child, Toe (Sergio), killed in a car accident when he was fifteen. The nickname traces to his birth as a baby so big that his older brother Diego said, "If we are all one foot, he's the big toe." Until now, thirteen years after his death, I have not seen Toe's grave or heard the story of the gravestone farther down the same row. His cousin, Fernando, was found with a bullet wound to his neck soon after Toe died. "He never got over Toe's death," Eva says. "He was his best friend. He would wait for him at school. One day, he was waiting and he asked me why Toe didn't come. '*Mijo*, he's dead,' I said, 'You know that he's dead.' Just a few months later, his cousin was dead, too. A hunting accident, they said." Eva shakes her head.

Eva points to the space above Toe's grave where a five-foot statue of Jesus Christ once stood. The clay figure now inhabits Eva's garden, welcoming visitors who come to be healed. Local teenagers who rampaged the graveyard after Toe's burial shot off the arms just above the elbow. The vandals damaged a number of gravesites. The Anglo families were compensated, Eva says, while hers was not. "The lady argued that they didn't have any more money to pay. How come she paid for the others? Was it because our tombstone was in Spanish? She wasn't able to explain."

The assault on the statue compounded the already unbearable loss. Worse still, Eva recalls, were the representatives of the Catholic group, Las Crucistas, who came to her door after the funeral. They reprimanded her for not crying at the service, her absent tears evidence that she was "not a Christian mother." Rumors circulated, too, that Toe had been adopted. Eva's eyes blaze with anger as she recalls that time. "The harm of death coming into my home and taking my child was already done. But the harm of people saying I was insensitive, that I was not a Christian mother, that my boy was not my child—all those gossipy stories hurt me more. Nobody said, 'Why didn't you cry?' so I could say, 'I had already cried' or, 'Because I was taught not to' or, 'Because I have to be standing on my own two feet for Martin, Cami, and all my other children. They have lives, too.'"

Toe died on June 6. The next day, the National Endowment for the Arts called Eva to announce her National Heritage Award for making *coronas*. "I couldn't take it in," she says, noting how often happiness and tragedy coincide. Toe was buried on Diego's birthday. His death devastated Eva's family. "We had a special relationship with that child," Eva says. "It was really bad for everyone, especially Marty. My son went through a lot for his brother's death. I believe this family is very special because they know things even before they happen. Chayo in Texas saw Toe; he went to Chayo before he left this earth. Martin was firefighting and he knew." Perhaps Toe knew as well. Weeks before his death, he gave Eva a collection of stories about his life. "He handed me that book, maybe two or three weeks before. He said, 'Here is my story, Mama, because you're going to read it. One of these days, you're going to read it.' So I read it in front of all the people and I didn't cry.'"

Eva's dry eyes were testimony, she says, to her faith. "I was up in the pulpit singing the praises to the Lord, 'This is the day that the Lord has made; let us rejoice in it, even if my heart is dying. I cannot make the great spirit a liar.'" Eva argues, "God knows how much pain we can take in. When Toe died, he [God] made me dumb; he dumbfounded me. God knew I wasn't going to be able to handle Toe's death. He was not just my son; he was my beautiful friend. How could I have been able to take that, his death, to see those eyes close forever? God knew it and he anaesthetized me so I could drink in the pain little by little, not *swoosh!* all at one time."

When Toe died, Eva summoned her experience of death at the time of Cami's birth. "I knew what death was. I saw it when I lived it, or died it, or whatever. I don't know what to call it, but it helped me. It's indescribably beautiful. It's not what people make it. Death helped me through my son's death. I couldn't cry and I wasn't going to pretend. I know my son is not gone. His body is gone but he's right here with me now. I have a picture of him on my altar. I have him every day, not only for Los Muertos day."

Cultural beliefs, Eva says, also influenced her failure to cry at the funeral. In her childhood, crying was taboo. "My mother would hit me and hit me and I would cry and she says, 'Don't cry.' But I have to cry because she's hitting me! But in the Aztec culture, you don't cry." Eva's parents endured years of poverty and dislocation; such hardships likely contributed to their stoicism. Eva exhibits a similar resolve in the face of ongoing travails. Yet, now she also displays emotions readily; she cries easily, flashes with anger when provoked, and always reaches out with love and affection. Her emphasis on a public show of strength at the funeral and other such stories tell us much about the complexity of death and reactions to it in pre-Columbian and contemporary Mexican culture.

Aztec culture is often described as fatalistic, ruled by an acceptance of one's predetermined fate. All death, including human sacrifice, was the return of a human debt to the gods. But many scholars find in Aztec thought a complex balance between individual free will and the determinism of a higher being. The *tlamatinime* (wise men) believed that an individual, "by controlling himself, could regulate his life."[1] Further, Aztec philosophy about life and death encompassed the celebration as well as the fatalism of *flor y canto*: "I weep, I feel forlorn;/I remember that we must leave flowers and songs/Let us enjoy ourselves now, let us sing now!/For we go, we disappear."[2]

To weep and to sing. Contemporary Mexicans respond to death with the full range of human emotion. Yet, the weeping and the singing seem curiously absent from many popular and scholarly works that describe the "Mexican view of death" as irreverent, indifferent, stoic. In *The Labyrinth of Solitude*, Octavio Paz writes that the Mexican looks at death "with impatience, disdain and irony." The Mexican of Paz's world "is familiar with death, jokes about it, caresses it, sleeps with it, celebrates it."[3] Scholar Stanley Brandes argues that this view should be carefully examined through ethnographic research. Paz's lyrical book-length essay is not, Brandes adds, drawn from research or observation of real communities in all their ornery variation. In fact, like human beings everywhere, Mexicans confront death differently based on region, ethnicity, age, class, and other factors.[4] Yet, even these critics agree that Mexican stoicism in the face of death is both real and mythic. Historically, tragic death from poverty, high infant mortality rates, and accidents contributed to a shorter life span. Improved health care and other changes altered that reality, yet the rituals created to face these assaults live on in Mexico. Surely they are evident in Eva's life.

One force behind the persistent rituals and beliefs is what some call Day of the Dead tourism. Government support originally emphasized states such as Michoacán, but the celebration of death now thrives everywhere. On November 1 and 2, tourists as well as locals fill cemeteries in Mexican and Mexican American towns. Graves teem with smiling sugar skulls, pink-frosted breads, and toys. The carnival atmosphere of the celebration especially fascinates those from countries where sobriety and silence dominate approaches to death. As the United States and Mexico grow more intertwined, Brandes argues, the Mexican view of death becomes "cultural capital." It helps create a distinct and separate Mexican national identity.[5]

In his argument against those who see Mexican attitudes as exotic or strange, Brandes underscores how similar European beliefs and practices once were. After the Black Death, the Grim Reaper appeared everywhere in Europe. In the sixteenth century, the essayist Montaigne wrote, "Let us remove death's strangeness and practice it instead."[6]

San La Muerte, also called Santa Muerte (Saint Death or Holy Death) represents a marriage of the Grim Reaper and folk beliefs throughout Latin America and Mexico. The figure originally appeared as an amulet used to injure or kill one's enemies. In his evolution to folk saint, San la Muerte became linked with healing and protection of life. Yet, beliefs about witchcraft and the "black arts" persist.[7] San La Muerte is revered by prisoners, drug traffickers, and other outlaw cultures as well as by devout law-abiding citizens. Eva feared San la Muerte until her brother Manuel sent her a figure of the saint with a story from his home in northern Mexico. A friend arrived on his doorstep one night bleeding from an assault by three men. He might have been killed had he not invoked San la Muerte. I finally meet Eva's La Muerte a few years after our visit to the cemetery. Skeletal bones form the figure's head and arms; gold robes adorn his body. "I'm getting to know him," Eva says as she introduces her new saint. "I talk to him in the morning, 'How are you today?' but I still think he's so ugly!" Eva invokes San La Muerte's presence only when absolutely necessary, never abusing his power.

As we linger on the cool granite stones in the Nyssa cemetery, Eva recalls her father's death—another occasion when her behavior raised eyebrows. As he lay dying in the hospital, his final words to Eva were, "'Genoveva, *voy con Dios*. I am going with God. I do not want you to cry. I am going to be separate from you, but I am not going to die. You are not going to a funeral; you are going to a party. You are going to sing. I want you all dressed in yellow.' He loved me in yellow. But I couldn't find a yellow dress, so I wore a pink blouse and a big bracelet, and I went dancing. And Jo, the big eyes, you know! One lady tells me 'I'm so sorry.' I say, 'I'm not sorry, I'm happy because my daddy's not suffering.'"

A slight breeze cools the sweat on my arms. Overhead and across the highway, crop dusters blanket the earth with a putrid-smelling dust. Even at a quarter mile distance, the pesticides burn the inside of my nostrils. Eva leads me to a row of infant graves clustered together. "These are the angels," she says, "who came to us for one day, one month, some even for a year." *Angelitos*, many believe, bypass purgatory to go directly to heaven. Eva recalls the rituals following the death of San Juanita, her mother's last child. "They made paper wings and put them on her, and they made a little *corona* of paper flowers and the shiny aluminum foil from cigarettes. They sang and it was so beautiful." This ritual called for singing, but Eva acknowledges the need to weep. Beneath the surface throbbed her mother's grief at losing yet another child. Perhaps, Eva mused once, such profound loss shaped the way she and her mother clashed. Maybe her mother couldn't risk a bond to Eva after the deaths of the five children.

The deaths of the *angelitos* who lie in the Nyssa cemetery also differ in important ways from that of Eva's youngest sibling. She points to specific gravestones, "That one to the left had no arms, this one twisted legs." She indicates a slab that slants to one side, its misshapen form mimicking the body it shelters. "She was born like a monster to my niece," Eva says. "No one did anything." Another grave holds the lost baby of her daughter Chayo, who worked in the fields until the day she delivered. The crop dusters swirl and moan. I don't need to ask Eva for her theory about the mangled babies. I have read about the estimated three hundred thousand farmworkers who suffer pesticide poisoning each year.[8] "Oh, Jo," Eva says, "there are so many stories."

Dusk descends. The zoom and rattle of old Chevys without mufflers rises behind us. Nyssa's youth arrive for a night of drinking and revelry—siblings, perhaps, to the kids who amputated the arms of Eva's Christ statue so many years before. As we descend into a slightly cooler Nyssa, Eva says, "For some times in your life, it's easy not to believe. For a while, I didn't. I would tell my friend, 'He says that he [God] has me in the hollow of his hand, well, I want him to throw me down. He's just watching me, putting all this stuff on me.' But it was just anger coming out of the body. I've seen dogs—and I learn a lot from animals that don't talk to you—they go into the water. Then they come out and shake themselves off. When wrong things come, we want to shake them off as soon as we can. But there's so much learning in there, even when it's really painful. Now I say, 'Lord, you took one away and it hurts like hell, but they're all yours. You just lent them to me. If you want all of them, take them. Just give me the power to go through it.' And he does. And I believe—through the thick and the thin."

During Toe's lifetime, the Castellanoz clan would have family meetings each week to talk about problems. Toe's role was truth teller, displaying a bit of Eva's *mula* spirit. When Ted was at home, he often reprimanded the family for scattering shoes around the living room; he, however, left his shoes wherever he chose. "Nobody could say anything," Eva recalls, "except Toe. He would say to Ted, 'Remember we had that meeting and you said nobody could leave their shoes in the living room? Well, put away your shoes.'"

After Toe's death, the idea of a family gathering chafed the raw wound. Then came the first Thanksgiving. The family placed a chair for Toe and cut him a piece of turkey. "We knew our life had to go on because he had taught us a lot. He taught us in different ways to say 'I love you.' We knew we loved each other but we didn't say the word. Now, one of my sons, a big fat man, thirty-five years old, holds his brother, kisses his cheek and says, 'I love you, brother.' Toe taught us. Death taught us."

12

Cutting the Onions

La Enfermedad: A *comadre* in Ontario came to
me after her son was killed in a car accident.
She couldn't sleep or eat, she didn't want to
live. Would it ever get better, she asked?

El Remedio: I reminded her about how we used
to work in the onion fields. Remember the
knife, how sharp it was for the first onions?
Then you cut and cut and it still goes through,
but it's not so sharp. That's how it will be.

IN A NAMPA, IDAHO, GRAVEYARD, the angel Gabriel inhabits the bottom left corner of a marble stone. He gazes upward
toward the image of a high-cheekboned beauty with a dazzling
smile captioned "Our Angel." The inscription reads: "Angie—
Maria Evangelina Castellanoz. June 9, 1981–May 19, 2003. Loving Mother, Daughter, and Sister."

At Angie's funeral, well-meaning acquaintances tried to console Eva about her granddaughter's death. "She's in heaven, in a better place," one woman suggested. Eva's response to religious pieties was rage: "There is no better place for a beautiful young woman than here on this earth with her children, celebrating life." Many people, including Angie, had foreseen the end of that celebration. Just weeks before, she had taken out a life insurance policy. She knew that her children, Abel Jr. ("A. J."), Maribel Alejandra ("Alej"), and Byanca ("Perty") would need support after the murder she long predicted finally happened.

Angie's husband, Abel, was still at large when news of her death traveled through the network of Eva's friends. I had never met Angie, but I know her father, Ralph, Eva's third child. I had been to Nampa, a predominantly Latino town just over the Idaho border. Soon, the full story hit regional headlines. Between May 14 and 16, 2003, Angie had called the Nampa Police Department Victim/Witness Division numerous times. No one responded. On the morning of the murder, Angie phoned her mother in a panic. A call had come from a phone booth—Abel's signature way of bypassing the court's restraining order. "Call the police," her mother insisted. "What can they do?" Angie responded wearily.

She had reason for despair. During the previous five years, Abel Leon had contact with the police fifty-nine times. Of the thirty-five charges of domestic violence, domestic rape, and stalking, twenty-seven were simply dismissed. Abel's violence had begun soon after high-school sweethearts Angie Castellanoz and Abel Leon Ramírez met. The record of his first arrest in 1998 cites domestic battery: "slapping causing bleeding, pushing, obstruction of making 911 calls, threats to come back and finish." Still, short spells of happiness punctuated the couple's years of marriage and raising three children. Angie planned to finish her high-school

degree at Nampa's alternative school for teen parents. Abel, who
had come to the United States from Mexico at age eleven, hoped
to become a permanent resident. After each arrest, he promised
Angie he would change. After each pledge to reform, he exploded
into another spasm of violence. Charges against him included
assault on his pregnant sister, Mayren; harassment and stalking
of Angie; violation of protection orders, theft, and possession of
methamphetamine.

The eruptions culminated on October 14, 2002, when Abel
entered the house and raped Angie. She harnessed her courage to
press charges. A Nampa police officer came to interview Angie;
her mother, Sylvia Flores, Ralph's ex-wife, was present. Both
women felt that the officer doubted Angie; both suspected that he
was "getting off" on the details. The rape and its aftermath trau-
matized Angie; she became an "uncooperative witness," refus-
ing to speak to a second officer. Seven more contacts with police
followed in the next two weeks, including charges of stalking,
numerous violations of protection orders, and harassing phone
calls. On October 30, Angie fled Abel's death threats for the area's
only domestic violence center, the Valley Crisis Center. But she
chafed under the rules, especially one that prevented her from seeing her children that evening. The next day, she returned home.

In the six months before her death, Angie moved, changed jobs,
and made plans to file for divorce, get custody of the children, and
leave the area. In her last civil protection order request, she wrote:
"I tried to tell myself he would change. He has—he has gotten
worse." What could prompt Abel to change if her love and that
of her children, if the probation and warnings—none had yielded
results? Drug treatment might have helped; drugs and/or alcohol
figure in 90 percent of domestic violence cases. Abel might have

gone to prison, which would have safeguarded Angie, her children, and other community members. But he never served time. Of all the charges filed against him, only two misdemeanor counts of domestic battery appeared on his record. He plea-bargained every serious charge to a lesser one.

May 19 dawned bright and sunny. Angie's mother, Sylvia, arrived to drive her to work. Abel was already in the house. Angie grabbed the children and raced toward the car. Abel put a gun to her head and forced her back inside. Angie screamed to her mother for help. Sylvia phoned the police on her cell, begging them to hurry. But it was already too late.

A year later, Eva and I drive from Nyssa across Highway 20 to Nampa. We pass rusted trailers, where women stand in the windows frying meat for tacos. Past signs in English and Spanish, fields of alfalfa and vegetable seeds unfold for miles. In Nampa, we stop at Albertsons to buy cold drinks and flowers for Angie's grave. Eva hesitates near the checkout stand and then adds a six-foot pink silk daisy to her cart. A few miles farther, the graveyard rests amid the deep green of a quiet residential neighborhood. "She was so beautiful," Eva muses as we approach. "People would just stop on the street and stare." Angie's brother Ricky praised his sister's diligence in working two jobs while attending school and raising three children. "Angie's beauty was evident," Ricky wrote after her death, "but it was her inner light, her living in accord with highest dignity, that made her admirable." We find the gravesite, still covered with faded flowers. Angie's married name "Leon" does not appear on the gravestone. Eva weeps quietly. She pokes a hole in the ground for the giant daisy, its silk edges radiating sunlight onto Angie's engraved image.

Angie's murder filled the news in the Oregon-Idaho border area for weeks. Widespread anger followed. Community members formed a task force of over sixty citizens. The report they compiled gave voice to the many people outraged by Angie's death. The summary of events underscores a vast community failure. The way Abel had slipped through the system, plea-bargaining serious charges to lesser ones, proved to be a prevailing pattern in Nampa and surrounding counties. The civil protection orders Angie had filed were, in one assessor's words, "flimsy as the paper they are written on" unless followed by a quick response.[1]

The report prompted changes, some with a degree of immediate success. A fatality review clause added to existing law ensured examination of domestic violence deaths. Schools developed new educational curricula. Revisions began to the civil protection order process. More local police pursued training in handling domestic violence incidents, which had been available but spotty. A Nampa Family Justice Center was created as a kind of "one-stop" site for dealing with the morass of legal, psychological, and other issues surrounding such violence. A second shelter with fewer restrictions opened in the county. However, an addendum to the citizens' report laments the slow pace of change in other areas. Most damning of all is an appendix that describes cases stunningly similar to Angie's—women buying life insurance, building their own coffins.

Eva smoothes the ground around the gravestone, rearranging the sea of floral bouquets. She and her family, especially Ralph, have come to Nampa many times to visit the grave; they have talked to the press, local authorities, and domestic violence advocates. Their dignified presence tamped down the racism threatening to erupt. "It was easy for a lot of people to blame them," says task force spokesperson Teri Ottens. "You know, 'Oh Hispanics, that's how they are. Macho men, the families aren't together.' But then the families came forward. They were educated and sophisticated and they stood strong and said, 'No more.' No one around here will forget the name of Angie Castellanoz Leon for a long, long time. And no one will forget the family. They did more to change the community's attitudes toward Hispanics than any other time anyone can remember."[2]

Abel Leon turned himself in less than two weeks after Angie's death; the publicity made escape impossible. His trial was set for September 7. As we leave the cemetery, I ask Eva what the best possible outcome might be. She shakes her head. "I don't know, Jo. Some are calling for the death penalty. When I see him, I want to put out claws like this." She cups her hand and simulates a long, vicious scratch through the air with her nails. "I don't like it that I feel this way, but I do."

The night before our trip to the cemetery, I arrived in Nyssa to find Eva watching television. We chatted for a while before Eva went to bed and I fell asleep on the couch. In the morning, I peeked into her room. She slept as the television buzzed. Often, Eva watches cultural programs on channels like Canal Once (Channel Eleven) Mexico's oldest public broadcasting network. But this morning's show followed Scott Peterson's trial for murdering his pregnant wife. When she woke, Eva told me this trial mesmerized her. She reminded me of a story she'd told me years before, for Angie's death wasn't her first experience with the aftershocks of domestic violence.

When Eva's children were young, she and her mother discovered that the husband of a Mexican friend, María, was beating her. They urged her to leave. Eva recalls María as kind and gentle, a good mother to her five children. One day, she simply disappeared. Eva went to the house. "He [her husband] saw us and says, 'Oh, she took off with somebody else.' 'And the baby?' 'Oh, she left him.'" Telling the story, Eva shook her head, "María never would have left that baby. So I started fussing and getting raucous. I went to the police station, to welfare, to the court. I went everywhere with a bunch of other women. The police said, 'Go home, you have no business here.' For about four years, we didn't know, but we knew, we knew!" In those four years, the father had enlisted his own kids in a series of robberies. When he was finally arrested, Eva convinced one of the children to go to the police. "Go now," she urged, "He's in jail. He can't hurt you." The police came. "They brought all those tractors out and they found her body—just about ten feet from the front door." The story unfolded: a gruesome murder by the husband, who then forced the children to help clean up the blood and bury their mother. Juan, one of the children who had attached himself to Eva's husband, Ted, came to live with the Castellanoz family.

Eva saw signs of his deep disturbance early on. "He would hit me because I wanted him to take a shower or bath or change his clothes. I was black and blue most of the time." Eva tried to compensate for all the hardships Juan had endured, giving him the best school clothes. But Juan was always jealous of the other children. "My kids suffered a lot. I suffered a lot," says Eva. When Juan hit adolescence, he began cutting the nipple sections out of the girls' bras and the crotches out of their panties. Eva brought the story to children's services. Their intervention complicated matters. Eva and Ted had kept Juan for five years at their own expense. "Nobody cared, nobody said anything." When the state began to pay for his care—$152 a month—they forbade Eva to take him to the fields. "We would go to the onions, for money and to learn.

They could give me a million dollars for him, but I would still take him to the fields." "The onions" formed a symbolic center for the Castellanoz family: a source of livelihood, a way to learn about cooperation and hard work, a rite of passage. When children's services prohibited Juan's work in the fields, they sought protection for a child. But for Eva, including Juan in the family system by going to "the onions" *was* a form of protection.

One night during an argument, Juan lunged at Eva. Diego arrived to find his mother on the floor. "Diego got on him and beat him up," Eva remembers. "Then children's services came, and they arranged for Juan to go to his sister's in Nampa for maybe three weeks. My kids were all standing there and they sang out all together, 'How about three years?' Diego was the foreman of the group and he said, 'Take him. Nobody's going to hit my mom.'"

The experience with children's services colored Eva's perception of government agencies. Later, she held jobs with public programs—at a day-care center, with the Oregon State University Extension Service, and many others. Still, clashes of values sometimes emerged, especially around the treatment of children. "In our culture, we do things that are not sexual abuse but could be taken by someone [outside the culture] for sexual abuse. We fondle our little ones. When I'm changing my little girl, I say, 'Oh, *qué bonitas cositas* [what beautiful things]!' How otherwise are they going to learn that their body is wonderful? I used to bathe my kids together, not the boys first, then the girls. How otherwise are they going to learn respect?"

In dealing with violence against women, Eva's gripe with the authorities is more about power than cultural difference. When the police failed to investigate María's disappearance, they affirmed Eva's belief that men in charge would never listen to a bunch of

Mexican women. Her *testimonio* reverberates outward to the many women and children who have suffered violence. When Angie's pleas for help went unheeded, old fears, resentments, and suspicion of racism surfaced. Domestic violence is widespread among all populations. But among Latinos, intersecting cultural forces are at work: poverty, racism, colonization, and homophobia. Treatment must consider all facets.[3]

Angie's death affected the entire community and profoundly disturbed Eva's sense of justice. "When some of the most awful things happen in our lives, I don't believe that it's only me that's hurt. The whole community is wounded." Of the tragic murder of Juan's mother and the lasting consequences, Eva says, "We were all lame, it happened to all of us." She could have been speaking for Nyssa and Nampa after Angie's death—or for any community in America.

We make our way back to Nyssa at dusk as the Latino workers in wide hats, some with children strapped to their backs, walk toward the highway. At Eva's, the pictures of Angie suddenly seem multiplied, her gorgeous smile illuminating the room as I fall asleep. The next day, Ralph drops off two of Angie's children on his way to work. They spend half their time with Sylvia in Nampa, the other half in Nyssa with Ralph. Both grandparents are deeply devoted to their care. Alej is quiet—a small version of her radiant mother. A. J. immediately falls asleep on a chair; his nights are too haunted for sleep. The family will keep his initials but eventually change his name from Abel Junior to Andres Josu. All three children will change their surname from "Leon" to "Castellanoz."

Later, we drive the kids to the trailer across from the sugar factory where Eva runs her youth program. A. J. runs for the trampoline that Eva found at a garage sale, begging us to watch. As he sails through the air, a spark of joy ignites his face. Eva lights up as well, as though for that instant, she has forgotten how choked with weeds his path will be on his way to clear ground.

On my final night in Nyssa, Eva and I lounge on the couch, talking about Angie's death. "Her husband who killed her has a counselor in prison, while I sit at home and weep. Who can afford eighty or ninety dollars an hour? That is why our people come to me. I can listen and it's free." She returns to the memory of her parents' loss, the iconic story that always surfaces when she considers lessons of life and death. "Losing five children, not having a home, being a person that drinks all the time, not having the money to save your kids, having to carry your dead little boy in a box, no place to bury him. Your other kid is dying, then you have two dead. So you're looking not only for a place to bury one little person, but two. Then three and four?" Eva fixes on the blue light of the television, perhaps pondering the workings of a mysterious God. For all the assaults Eva has endured, she invokes a benevolent view of death. She says of her parents' beliefs, "They always thought, '*Ya no sufrir mas*'—no more suffering. The final healing."

Can there be a final healing when death stems from an enraged man rather than a mysterious God? As I leave Nyssa, Angie's image travels with me, and I wonder if the edge of this knife will ever dull for Eva.

13

The Mexican Jacuzzi

La Enfermedad: This problem with the blood—
the Big C—she's strong and fat and powerful—a
great big person knocking outside the door.

El Remedio: I refuse to answer so she cannot
come in. I don't say the word. Maybe some
people call this denial. But I pretend and maybe
the pretending makes me believe. So that's what
I do for the men and women who come.

BY 1994, SEVERAL YEARS HAVE PASSED since Eva's diagnosis of the "problem in the blood." Driving along the Columbia River to eastern Oregon, I ponder what it means to be seriously ill—and how it might feel to outlive doctors' predictions of your death. I arrive in Nyssa in late afternoon. Rain clouds darken the onion fields across from Eva's house. She emerges, arms outstretched to hug me. A streak of sun breaks through, illuminating her face. A band holds back her ebony hair, accenting her high cheekbones and radiant skin. Relief fills me at seeing such obvious good health. Always, I'm a little amazed at Eva's powers of self-renewal. How has she kept this illness at bay?

As we sit under the shade of the towering locust tree, I ask tentatively, "You've been well?" Eva pauses. In response, she circles her illness with a story about its possible source. "When I was growing up, I was so skinny! I needed strength. My daddy would break open beef bones with a rock," she says. "Nobody could have the bone marrow; it was mine. Now, I think back to those days and I say, what an irony."

We don't talk directly about Eva's illness because *el remedio* depends on coded speech. "I don't even mention the name," says Eva. "The Big C—she's strong and fat and powerful, a great big person knocking outside the door, but I do not answer. It's like my friend Marie when she comes to visit. If I open the door, she can come in. If I don't, she can't."

Eva remembers when the stigma of the Big C was used against her. At the time of her diagnosis, the Baker Catholic Diocese had awarded her a grant to study theology and sociology at Portland State University. Upon completion, she would receive a certificate to practice youth ministry. "When people found out I was sick, that word, they threw me in the trash can. They didn't send me the books anymore or the letters about when the meetings were going to be. You know, they thought, 'She's gonna die, she's not worth the money we're going to spend on her.' This is what I believe. Maybe it's not true but nobody bothered to tell me [if it wasn't true]. It hurt me to be put aside and I haven't been picked up anymore."

Eva has sought many forms of treatment. Inside the house hangs a Native American drum left by a healer who came to perform a ceremony. A group of Eva's friends raised money for the drum rit-ual. She has undergone extensive chemotherapy at a Boise hospital and returns for frequent checkups on her remission. She uses the prayers and herbal treatments she learned from her mother. On this trip, I begin to understand an additional factor—the central role that language and ritual play in Eva's self-healing.

One day during my visit, Eva decides to show me the places where she goes to keep the big fat woman outside the door. Irri-gated fields of flowers give way to parched desert as we leave Nyssa in the early morning. We pass through small towns where the tav-erns' weathered signs hawk "booze and grub." Past red-rock can-yons, a gravel road leads into the Owyhee Mountains. We park and ascend a winding path. Scrambling over scree, we finally arrive at an open expanse. Huge rounded stones cover the earth, eroded to a high sheen of muted red, light ash-green, and a shim-mering gray-gold. This is Eva's "Pregnant Earth." We drape our bodies over the rocks, soaking up their life-giving heat.

Time suspends as we lie in the sun. Then Eva leads me toward a cairn of stacked stones. The mountain air is cool, the twisting path dotted with Indian paintbrush and wild iris. Beyond the tower of rocks lies a glistening pool of turquoise water. "Here it is," Eva announces, smiling broadly, "the Mexican Jacuzzi." She wears a white cotton skirt, which billows up around her waist as she lowers herself into the natural hot spring. "I believe the water is sacred. I say for it to cleanse me. It has all the Pine-Sol and Clo-rox and all the things you disinfect with." Her joyful expression evokes her photo at age sixteen, before illness ravaged her body, before the years of chemotherapy, before all the death and loss.

In her passage from illness and pain, Eva has relied on meta-phor, which literally means to "transfer" or "carry across." From our first visit, Eva's powerful use of creative language stunned me. In her everyday speech, metaphors such as "Catholicism is a dress that doesn't fit" startle us into "seeing differently." For years, I've watched her teach through symbols, lining up the green and ripe tomatoes to instruct about sexuality. But it's only now that I see connections between metaphor in daily life, in poetry, and in ritual and healing.

For the poet, metaphor "carries across" meaning. In stating that something is something else, the speaker or writer creates a new entity. Metaphors range from the prosaic—the sunset is a peach split over the horizon—to the surprising— a maraschino cherry amid healthy food is a "stripper at a social club."[1] But metaphor's transformative power goes beyond poetry to form the bedrock of our language and conceptual system. In a classic example, linguists George Lakoff and Mark Johnson show how the concept that "argument is war" underlies and reflects a world of thought: we "shoot down" or "demolish" points of "attack," end up "right on target," make "indefensible" claims. To see how deeply engrained such metaphors are, they argue, imagine instead a culture in which argument is a dance.[2]

As I dangle my legs in the Mexican Jacuzzi, I muse on Eva's creativity in her work as a healer and in her own recovery. When she is rebirthed by the earth or refuses entry to the big, fat woman at the door, she does more than use figurative speech. She wards off her disease. When Eva dips into the Mexican Jacuzzi, she turns it from an ordinary natural hot springs into the spiritual cleanser she requires. "Some people call me crazy," Eva says about her beliefs, "and I might be, but it has worked for me. So why not for others?"

Healers in many cultures use metaphor in their rituals, linking symbols to bodily experience and to a broader cosmology. Among the Songhay of Niger, the healer or *sorko*, must master the metaphors of ritual texts; these teach him to control the invisible forces of the Songhay universe, protect his community, and more effectively heal. The *sorko* learns this wisdom through following a metaphoric "road" that forms their cosmos.[3] In the world of Eva's Nahuatl-speaking ancestors, the wise men, or *tlamatinime*, were philosophers and scientists as well as healers. They used the rhythms of poetry to help remember and preserve scientific knowledge. A wise man was described as one who "comforts the people . . . helps, gives remedies, heals everyone."[4] Poetic metaphor expressed life's inevitable pain; its beauty offered a respite from that pain. *"Although it be jade, it will be broken/although it be gold, it will be crushed."*[5]

Metaphor can be both oppressor and liberator. Susan Sontag's *Illness as Metaphor* explores how metaphoric thinking can be turned against the patient. Sontag compares the nineteenth-century view of tuberculosis sufferers as creative, romantic souls with contemporary beliefs about cancer patients as emotionally stunted, repressed personalities who bring on their disease. Illness is not a metaphor, she argues, but a set of physiological symptoms. But patients of all kinds also call on metaphor, as Eva does, for transformation. Chemotherapy patients seek symbols for the potent chemicals coursing through their veins; some imagine warriors battling the diseased cells.[6] Psychologists and psychiatrists urge patients toward renewed vision through imaginative language. We need metaphor, one scholar argues, because the healing process is "hampered by the concreteness of our language."[7] Healing yokes mind and body to make meaning of experience. Metaphor serves as a bridge between our cultural narratives and the body's story, between healer and patient, between the sick person and the imagined state of wellness.

Watching Eva in the clear hot pool, I imagine her crossing over, if only for a moment, to that promised land of health. She appears calm, released from the worries of daily life by the hot springs, by the sun and the tranquil setting. But more importantly, she has slipped into a ceremony of renewal. In ritual, we leave the world behind to stand at the door of possible transformation. Once we experience this state, we hunger to do so again. I briefly surrendered to such a crossing when Eva performed a *limpia* for me. I remember the power of the symbols she used: the purple cloth she draped over my body; the burning sage and bay incense; the recitation of prayers to "let the sun melt my pain." A lightness of spirit enveloped me. Ritual affects us as poetry does, by enacting change through symbols. The sensation of being "moved" is at once bodily, psychic, and for some, spiritual. When Eva stands you at the window to fill your cup with sunshine or beckons the Clorox in the Mexican Jacuzzi to disinfect you, she is calling on metaphor's "suggestive magic."[8]

To those who dismiss traditional healing as hocus-pocus, Eva just shrugs. "I talk to my body and my body listens. Maybe the pretending makes me believe. So that's what I do for the men and women who come. I say, 'Think about something else. Give yourself a new name, give your illness something nicer. Pretend like a child.'"

Eva's "pretending" builds on her own faith and what she gleans from others. "I have a little faith and I borrow a lot," she often says. Today, she expands that concept to explain that she gains power from those she serves. "People trust their lives to my care," Eva says. "I can't bottle that. I can't box it, but it helps me." That trust engenders the strength she needs to help others cross over to health.

We rest quietly at the edge of the water, letting the afternoon sun dry our clothes. I'm reluctant to leave this peaceful place but we finally make our way down the mountain path. Sloping sunlight illuminates the Pregnant Earth as we pass, saturating the color of the green and gold rocks. Below, the valley unfolds. Eva's dress has bleached to a radiant white; her face glows. "These are my healers," Eva says, waving a hand back toward the Mexican Jacuzzi and Pregnant Earth. Her statement encompasses the natural elements, her faith in God and other people, and the power of imaginative language to mediate between worlds. As we begin the drive back to Nyssa, Eva returns to metaphor to explain what illness, death, and loss—the "children too big to carry"—have taught her. "I need the child I couldn't carry because he's so big. I had to have death so that I can understand. If you want to call me anything, call me a wounded healer. I am wounded before I am going to try to heal a wound."

In 2002, I learn that Eva has suffered a stroke. A few days later, I'm en route to Nyssa when an oil spill closes my usual route across I-84. I detour south toward John Day and the desert outside Burns. Passing the Owyhee Mountains, I remember the Mexican Jacuzzi with longing. But I banish the thought of stopping, remembering that Eva holds dinner until a guest arrives. I push my speed to seventy but still arrive hours late. From the driveway, I already smell the fried meat and tortillas. Eva sits out back with her family, who has indeed waited for me. She looks a bit thinner but otherwise healthy. Xochitl clowns in the backyard. We laugh and talk over our meal of pozole and tacos until everyone heads home. Then,

Eva's eyes fill as she talks about Xochitl's health problems. She worries about her son Marty, now in Iraq. "How can I close my heart? The doctors say not to worry, not to take so much in. How can I not feel?"

Eva describes the stroke and her eventual recovery. "I was in a Wal-Mart store with Maria and Xochitl. I went to the bathroom, and Jo, everything cut loose—vomit, urine, it was horrible. I couldn't have my daughter see me like that. I cleaned myself up and went to the car. We went home and I lay down. When I got up to get a sweater because of the chill, I saw my face!" She described her tearing eyes, her drooping face and slack mouth. She knew she'd had a stroke, but she feared seeking help. "Why, Jo? Why don't I get what I need? Is it because I remember my mother, how she was scared to go for help, scared because we were wetbacks?"

Eva finally went to the hospital with her son. They waited for hours in the emergency room. When an attendant wheeled her in for an MRI, the nurse asked about insurance. "I have only $150," said Eva. The nurse moved aside to consult with the doctor, leaving Eva to wonder if they would perform the MRI. Now, the $750 bill waits. Eva unfolds a note someone sent her about the recent stroke of a friend. He is still in the hospital, with only partial recovery of his speech. Eva expresses sadness for his suffering; she also notes that he got top-notch care. Maybe, Eva says, she recovered more rapidly than her friend because "God knows I have nothing. He gives me what I need."

As we get ready for bed, I tell Eva about my yearning as I passed the russet rocks of the Owyhee Mountains. "I loved going to that Mexican Jacuzzi," I recall. "Maybe we could go back sometime." Her face falls. "They closed it off. Some bad things happened there. People say there was a rape, maybe a suicide, too. They put up a barrier so now we can't go anymore." I pause a moment, wondering if Eva needs the waters now. She looks renewed; it's hard for me to imagine that she recently had a stroke or that the Big C still threatens her life. "Do you feel like you're healed?" I ask. I'm not even certain what I mean: recovered from the stroke, from the illness we cannot name, or from the many forms of pain in her life.

Her answer reminds me that healing never depended on the Jacuzzi waters alone. Healing happens in the "crossing over," in the connections between people, between interior beliefs and places and objects in the world. "I don't look this way because I'm not sick," she says. "I look this way because I believe in the things that can't be seen. I cannot explain to you why I am able to get up. But I look into your eyes and I see a promise and a hope."

PART III

The Dream

I'd rather be a poor man in America
than a millionaire in Mexico.

—FIDEL SILVA

Nyssa was my daddy's dream.
I want to be part of the realization of that dream.

—EVA CASTELLANOZ

Un Mestizaje Nuevo: "An identity that is shaped by both cultures
yet possesses neither culture in its entirety."

—JOHN FRANCES BURKE,
MESTIZO DEMOCRACY: THE POLITICS OF CROSSING BORDERS

14

My Piece of the Puzzle

La Enfermedad: If I'm hurt, the whole of Nyssa
is hurt because that little blood vessel, or that
little toe or finger is hurt. We are one body.

El Remedio: I gave Nyssa nine wonderful
people, and Nyssa helped me nourish my
children. So we're great partners.

ON A BRIGHT SUMMER MORNING, sunflowers fill the window of Eva's casita, rising from the garden that stretches behind to the Snake River. Her son Diego stands outside near the driveway. I haven't seen Eva's eldest son for five or six years, busy as he has been with family, work, school board, and other activities. It's 2006, two years since Diego finished his term as mayor of Nyssa, freeing him to spend more mornings helping Eva. All her sons—Ricky, Ralph, Marty, and Cami—tend the cattle out back. Before he enters, Diego peers in the window, his face framed by the brilliant flowers. It's a fitting image for the "golden" child that Eva calls "the father of this family." "He helped me bring up his brothers and sisters," she says. "He has seen us through thick and thin." .

As he sits down to tortillas, my eyes dart back and forth between his face and a photo hanging on an adjacent wall. Next to Diego, a bit stooped by age, stands Eva's father. Fidel Silva's shock of white hair contrasts with his grandson's dark youth. Today, Diego's hair has grayed slightly, but otherwise he appears unchanged—clear brown eyes, a wide handsome face, and heavy brows that recall his father, Ted. As Diego describes his plans for the day, my eyes fix on the dual portrait. Though both men look straight at the camera, a current of connection runs between them. Eva doesn't need to turn to the photo, for she sees her father in her son, the dream realized two generations later.

Eva can't say exactly why her father had his sights set on Nyssa from his first experience as a contract worker here in the 1940s. Perhaps the Owyhee Mountains resembled the hills beyond Valle de Santiago in Mexico. Maybe he'd grown fond of living near the Rio Grande in Texas, making the nearness of Oregon's Snake River alluring. But Fidel Silva's fierce determination to make this town home transferred to Eva. She doesn't analyze why she loves Nyssa. That would be akin to asking why you cherish and care for your own body.

Cruising down Thunderegg Boulevard into Nyssa, I note recent additions—the Koffee Korner espresso shop and a tanning salon that promises to "Sun Your Buns." The town Fidel Silva found when he arrived to stay in 1957 is hard to conjure. Eva remembers several flourishing bakeries, four banks, five or six clothing stores, a theater, and Mexican dances every weekend night. The migrant population swelled each spring through the harvest season. On this sleepy summer afternoon, a sense of fallen splendor prevails. Boards cover the front of one shop; "For Sale" signs adorn others. In the window of Mint Alley, mannequins in 1950s polyester dresses lean back as though the past might support them. On a side street, the beet growers association stands across from the Oregon Trail Agricultural Museum. The old Hotel Western houses part of the museum; its washed brick façade reveals the grandeur of Nyssa's past. To an outsider, the "Thunderegg Capital," named for the abundant geodes in the area, feels frozen in time.

"I don't know what happened," Eva says of the economic downturn. "Things just started to close." Some trace the town's decline to the creation of I-84, the interstate link between Portland and Boise. Prior to its completion in 1980, traffic had to pass through Nyssa, which kept downtown flourishing. But the town's life is not so much absent as hidden. Nyssa's beauty mirrors the thundereggs, the nondescript brown rocks that crack open to reveal startling patterns. Many in Nyssa express a sense of strong community spirit. After nearly forty years of teaching English at Nyssa High School, Clyde Swisher chose to retire here. He insists that the town is "not dying on the vine." Cleta DeBoer, who works for the chamber of commerce, admits that "the economy is not great, but people still pull together." Librarian Kate Adams points to how well Nyssa functions with a limited resource base; she also sees expansion ahead. Nyssa may become one of the circles of concentric growth outward from the Boise area. Adams notes the increasing number of people applying for library cards. Many live in outlying areas, drawn to rural and small-town community life.

Latinos are the greater part of the Nyssa community. At the M&W Market, the daunting variety of corn and flour tortillas, salsas, and spices reflects Nyssa's future. Over 57 percent of the population is Latino, though their presence feels stronger to the casual observer. Of Nyssa's 3,195 residents, 39 percent are under fifteen, making Nyssa a town of young families, including those of Eva's children.

Later in the afternoon, Eva and I drive through town. Paint peels and foundations sag on some of the small wood-frame houses we pass. But not those of Eva's children. Most of them are still at work, but we tour the outside of their homes. "They all take such good care of their houses and gardens," Eva brags. "My boys especially. Everything must be just so." As we reach Ricky's house, Eva exclaims, "Look!" His open garage door reveals shelves of neatly stacked supplies. "The other kids even give him a hard time, it's so perfect. And when his wife, Yolanda, pulls into the drive- way, he has her plate on the table. He's the husband I was raising my boys to be." As we swing by the M&W for groceries, she says, "I don't have nine children. I have one of each. My children are not perfect," she adds, though I sense she doesn't believe it, "but each is a treasure." Eva has realized her father's dream in this mantle of family that surrounds her. The Castellanoz clan is grounded, not to be dislodged.

The Cayuse and Paiute Indians once inhabited the land on which Nyssa now stands. Fur trappers likely trekked through this region in the early nineteenth century. Many Oregon Trail emi- grants came west at Snake River Crossing, a site now marked by a kiosk a few miles south of Nyssa. The 1860s gold rush lured miners; railroad workers followed when the Oregon Short Line

Railroad opened in 1883. A bit north, a budding settlement called
Arcadia competed with Nyssa for population and commerce. In
1903, Nyssa incorporated. Perhaps, one local history muses, Nyssa's "free spirit" trumped Arcadia's controlled atmosphere as a
company town. A 1911 brochure hailed Nyssa as a "progressive
and growing city." It urged readers to consider the region's farm-
ing potential, claiming, "there is room for all of us."[1] Space was
plentiful, water less so until 1932. The 417-foot Owyhee Dam
made irrigated land a draw for Dust Bowl refugees in the 1930s.
The federal Farm Security Administration further enticed settlers with loans during the Great Depression. Japanese Americans worked the farms through World War II to avoid internment
in camps, as did German prisoners of war. As agricultural land
expanded, Mexican workers filled labor shortages, culminating
in the Bracero Program, which brought Fidel Silva north.

Four distinct rivers flow into the Treasure Valley surrounding
Nyssa: the Snake, the Malheur, the Owyhee, and the Payette. The
local Four Rivers Cultural Center takes the waterways as a metaphor to celebrate the varied ancestries of the region's inhabitants:
Basque and other European groups, Native American, Latino, and
Japanese. Traces of each linger in the area but the Latino presence
feels most pronounced. From the vaqueros who came north from
California and Texas in the mid-1800s through the farmworkers
steadily migrating today, Nyssa has had a Mexican face.

When Eva and I return to the house, Diego is out back again, com-
pleting tasks left unfinished that morning. Eva speaks with pride
about his leadership roles. Diego expresses satisfaction with his
time as mayor of Nyssa. But he's also grateful that he can now
concentrate his energy on his wife, Cece (Cecelia), and their seven

children, their grandchildren, the school board and Nyssa City Council, and his job. From here, he's headed to the Amalgamated Sugar Company on Highway 82, a quarter mile from the Idaho border. Most of Eva's family has worked in the Nyssa processing plant, establishing a veritable dynasty. Diego rose to a supervisory position—a complex role in a tight-knit community where being the boss to friends and kin creates numerous challenges.

The original Amalgamated Sugar Factory opened in 1915, processing beets into White Satin sugar; it quickly became the largest employer in the area. Work in the fields, picking the crops, drew Mexican workers north; work at the factory sustained them. In 1994, a farmers' cooperative, the Snake River Sugar Company, formed to buy out the original company. In 2005, the plant closed because of NAFTA rules affecting white sugar. Production moved to Idaho; only brown sugar is still processed in Nyssa. The remaining skeletal crew includes Diego. Downsizing the Nyssa plant eliminated hundreds of jobs and stripped the community of almost a million dollars a year, including four hundred thousand dollars for the school system.

Diego fought the closure on every front. Google "Diego Castellanoz" and you'll find him at a meeting of the Free Trade Association or the International Labor Communications Association. He'll turn up at the University of Portland to speak out against CAFTA (the Central American Free Trade Agreement). "These trade agreements," says Diego, "craft a new way that companies do business. There is nothing fair about them." In voicing fears about CAFTA and local job loss, he says, "By all means, let's help our neighbors. But, let's help ourselves first."[2]

"Ourselves" is the community of Nyssa, where the median income is $28, 919 for a family, 19.9 percent of whom live below the poverty line; 28.2 percent of those affected are children. Plant closures force workers back to the fields. Eva laments that shift, despite her pride in the work ethic that "the onions" instilled in her children. Each has thrived, financially and socially. Eva celebrates their resourcefulness in all realms of work. But Eva acknowledges that advances in education and training catapult Latinos to new lives. "I see people on the street now, at the store, at the doctor's office, and I say, 'Good for you. You're not in the fields. You found out that you could learn.'"

A return to the fields from the factory also creates competition with the undocumented workers farmers can hire for lower wages. Between 50 and 70 percent of all migrant laborers in Oregon in 2006 worked without papers. Even documented workers don't receive health care, overtime, and other union-won benefits a factory worker enjoys. Many live in substandard housing and suffer discrimination. In addition to the harsh conditions, they risk neurological damage from pesticides. Those without health-care coverage, especially undocumented workers, rarely report symptoms. For all of these reasons, the average life expectancy for a migrant worker in 1998 was forty-eight years.[3] When Diego speaks out on these issues, his voice deepens with ancestral memory: years in the fields, his mother's determination, his grandfather's pride in making this place home.

Does the success of Eva's children mean that there is in fact "room for all" in the Treasure Valley? Room, perhaps, but it's not yet Arcadia for everyone. "It happens almost every day," Eva says of discrimination. "They look at the color. You stand and you don't get taken care of. You sit and nobody sees you. A lot of people don't know because it doesn't happen to them." She tells of helping a young blonde Mexican woman who had come to Nyssa and spoke no English. When Eva accompanied her to a medical appointment, the receptionist greeted the blonde woman warmly, ignoring Eva. As she recounted this story, Eva's voice sharpened with indignation. She was, after all, the long-time resident, the translator; she was also the older, dark woman.

Eva's story triggered a memory from one of my visits years before. One summer day, we went shopping at a mall in Ontario. Eva needed a basal thermometer to help a young woman monitor her temperature during ovulation. At the checkout, the smiling young clerk offered me a discount card. I didn't want to hassle with the forms, so the clerk simply swiped a card she had behind the counter, and $2.50 disappeared from my bill. Eva followed, paying full price for her thermometer and other items. Walking out to the car, Eva hung her head. I asked her what was wrong. "Do you see?" her voice quivered. "They will always prefer you. Did you see?" In fact, I hadn't. Perhaps this was a small sting, the failure to offer Eva the discount. But it ignited deeper cumulative pain. I wondered how many such slights I had missed over the years. How much collective noticing would it take to heal those wounds and move our communities toward wider change?

Later, Eva said, "I still like, even love Nyssa. I like its subtleness, its quietness. It gave me life and I gave it life. I gave Nyssa nine wonderful people, and Nyssa helped me nourish my children. So we're partners. We're great partners. I love her. If it's a woman, I love her. If it's a man, whatever. We helped each other." This particular partnership has not been without hardships, but Eva knows how to heal from difficult relationships.

I wake at dawn in Eva's casita the next morning and stumble outside to brush my teeth. The casita still lacks running water and other amenities but the space brims with warmth: lace doilies and fountains, dozens of miniature Mexican pots and ivy-stenciled cupboards in the kitchen. I splash water from a small cup on my face; it still smells of apples from the big drum of bathwater Eva heats in the sun under her apple tree. The droplets form a prism for the color that surrounds me: sunflowers waking to first light, the llamas' white wool coats, the garden of flaming bishop's plume and overflowing zucchini and other greens. A peacock struts next to the birdhouse. Roosters crow. My body shivers with life. Here is a piece of Fidel and Conchita Silva's Mexico in a western United States town. Eva has forged what some call "Mexicanidad"— creating and re-creating Mexico in memory, family, and community, even while forging a new identity in the United States.[4] In her impassioned defense of other immigrants, Eva pleads for their right to shape this hybrid culture and to flourish in a chosen place—their Arcadia.

I leave Eva reluctantly, but I need to get back to Portland before the heat intensifies. At the edge of town, I stop for a cup of tea at a twenty-four-hour gas station and convenience store. The young white woman, perhaps twenty, looks at me blankly.

"We don't sell tea."

"Is there a restaurant in town open this early?" I point toward Nyssa, whose center is a few blocks away.

"Oh, I don't know," she wrinkles her nose. "I never go there."

Eva refuses to gloss the racism she has encountered; she keeps alive the fissures and knotty truths of her history. Though her place is established in Nyssa, she knows how it feels to be seen as "other" or not seen at all. Because she remembers those afflictions, she links her destiny to that of other Latinos struggling to gain a foothold. "God could have put me in Portland," she said once during a discussion of immigration. "He could have put me in Pocatello, but he put me in Nyssa to be supported by the people here. I belong on this piece of the puzzle. If I'm hurt, the whole of Nyssa is hurt because that little blood vessel, or that little toe or finger is hurt. We are one body."

15

Ask Me

La Enfermedad: We did encounter a lot of
discrimination in school. I will hold them accountable
until the day I die for my kids not graduating.

El Remedio: We can make people prisoners
of a situation forever and that's not right.
They can change and we can help them.

"ENTERING BULLDOG COUNTRY," emblazoned in bright
blue letters on the side of Nyssa High School, greets visitors to
town. Just off Thunderegg Boulevard, the complex of primary and
secondary schools holds a central place in the landscape. When I
arrive to see Eva in early fall 2006, posters adorn the school lawn.
Some welcome students back to class. Others invite locals to foot-
ball games, a Saturday night lawn-mower race, a fiesta for teens,
and a Sunday morning pancake breakfast.

There is, it seems, much to celebrate. Over the past two decades,
Nyssa schools have battled high dropout rates and myriad social

problems to become one of the most lauded districts in Oregon. The elementary school outpaces the rest of the state in reading and math benchmarks; averages are in the 90 percent range in all areas. The middle school, cited for low scores in 2001, now rates "strong." Nyssa High made an exponential shift from a 42 percent dropout rate in 1998 to a little over 5.5 percent in 2005.

I've read about these shifts, wondering at how teachers can raise test scores without becoming slaves to the mandates of the No Child Left Behind Act. Nyssa schools are a microcosm of state and national education trends.[1] Everyone agrees that we need some kind of student assessment, but which tools actually measure change? Overreliance on standardized tests can distort and narrow the curriculum; testing also poses problems for low-income students and those who do not speak English as their first language.[2] These questions are particularly important for Nyssa schools, with their high percentages of both types of students.

I'm thinking aloud about these issues as we sit out back at Eva's on a balmy September day, the garden a golden backdrop. "Who should I talk to about the Nyssa schools?" I turn to Eva as she enters the birdhouse to feed the finches and cockatiels. "Ask me!" she declares, eyes blazing, for Eva has a different version of No Child Left Behind. In fact, only one of her nine children, Chayo, wore a cap and gown on graduation day.

"We did encounter a lot of discrimination in school," Eva fumes. "I will hold them [the school] accountable until the day I die for my kids not graduating!" She quickly adds, "Not that it matters, for they have done well. But now a piece of paper is needed for you to go anywhere. My kids should have gotten it, but they didn't because of the teachers. They had a meeting with one of the teachers right here, and every one of them told him how they'd been discriminated against—even in music! And my kids are very musical." Eva admits her children's weaknesses as well as their strengths. "My kids are very smart; they may not be readers and they acknowledge it. They cannot sit still for long periods. They are technical people; they are 'doing' people. But they are very truthful. They acknowledge their mistakes."

Nationally, Latinos drop out at a rate three times that of Caucasian students. Academic tracking into technical fields, lack of teacher involvement, and inadequate counseling all contribute to the high dropout rate. When teachers have low expectations, students produce the expected behavior and the cycle continues.[3] Eva's son Toe fit this pattern. His older siblings had struggled; by the time Toe got to school, his defenses were up. "He was the eighth," Eva recalls of this beloved son. "He told us, 'They're not going to do to me what they did to the rest.' He would tell them [the teachers], 'I'm gonna give you something to worry about.' He walks into the classroom the first day of school and says [to the teacher], 'I'm going to see to it that you don't last in this class two weeks.' That same day, he comes home and warns me, 'Mama. I'm going to give him hell because if he doesn't want me there, I'm not gonna learn.'"

To stanch the flow of Latino dropouts, education specialists call for multiple changes: greater commitment of teachers and staff, peer counseling, the development of role models. Many emphasize parental involvement; the summons to parents, however, isn't enough without outreach. Eva encouraged her children and helped them with homework, but she did not regularly go into the schools. Caring for her own nine children and others from the neighborhood consumed her time. She had other reasons as well. "I was very shy at the time. I didn't want to be seen because I felt I was ugly. I wasn't dressed like other people; I didn't have shoes.

I didn't want to embarrass my kids." Latino parents stress education yet many don't participate in school life. "I trusted the lives
of my kids and their futures to teachers," Eva laments, "because
this is how Mexicanos are. I was also taught by my parents, 'Your
teachers are like your parents in school.'" Such trust in educated
professionals is a working-class pattern as well as a Mexican one.[4]
Now, Eva says, "I regret that I never went in." She feels that she
might have come to understand the teachers' point of view as well.
"I didn't want to give my kids the wings to be rude and awful to
the teachers. They can make mistakes, too, they're human."

During the years that Eva was raising children, Nyssa was
slowly evolving into a predominantly Latino community. Along
with the growing pains, racist stereotypes multiplied. "We were
poor. Plus, my husband got into a lot of things—women. But he
wasn't a lazy person. We were never on welfare—never! He always
worked, but you get this label put on you and it stays." Eva drums
a knife on the picnic table as she describes those early years. The
pain is still palpable.

In 2000, Don Grotting, the current Superintendent of the Nyssa
Schools, took over. Transformation was in order. He said, "It took
a lot of trust to admit we were not doing the job correctly. We had
to ask what we needed to do to help these kids. If we had not been
willing to do that, things would not have changed." The schools
in Nyssa had to go to "where the students are," a move Eva sees
as critical. Changes happened on a structural and curricular level:
smaller class size, smaller student-teacher ratios, careful tracking
of students, a full-day kindergarten based on the needs of families without day care, new reading programs, and other reforms.
The number of Latino teachers in Nyssa also grew in the decade
between 2000 and 2009 from two to nine.

But the more important shift was attitudinal. Nyssa teachers now offer students what Eva believes her children didn't get:
faith in their abilities. Elementary school principal Geno Bates
says, "Teachers here have a belief system. They believe the kids
can learn and they know we believe in them."[5] That philosophy
applies to all students, say school officials, regardless if they're
still learning English or come from poor families. Such students
need special attention, argues Nyssa High School vice-principal
Luke Cleaver. He acknowledges the difficulties parents face. "If
you come from a non-English-speaking family, the chances that
you can be an advocate for your son or daughter are small. We
need to consider that."[6]

Diego Castellanoz has served many years on the school board;
he confirms that attitudinal changes were the catalyst. "Caring,"
he says, "is what helps the kids get through." At Nyssa High,
where 37 percent of the students come from migrant families, Principal Ken Ball says, "We're committed to following every student
before they get frustrated." One teacher changed her schedule so
she could stay late with a student who worked night shift, thus
making it possible for him to remain in school.

Nyssa teachers and administrators admit that they have not
yet reached their goal of full equity. "We don't want to see any
discrepancy between kids based on gender, ethnicity, or anything
else," Cleaver says. "We're not there yet, but we're working on it."
A further goal is increased college attendance, an area where Latinos currently lag behind the overall population.

Eva still laments the education her children didn't get. Entry
into the Oregon State University (OSU) Extension Service changed
her own life. In 1969, she began eleven years of training and work
as a nutritional aid. OSU hired her at thirteen dollars an hour—

a job that catapulted Eva out of the fields. At first, Ted wouldn't allow her to work outside the home. But Mrs. Barton, one of the OSU administrators, believed in Eva's potential. She helped negotiate a compromise: Eva would begin work but be home each day at noon to have Ted's lunch on the table. Her initial six-week training was augmented by weekly supplemental trainings. Once a year, she journeyed seven hours by car to Corvallis in the Willamette Valley for continuing education. "I was very, very privileged to be trained," Eva says. "Before that, it was a dark world for me. I wasn't good. I wasn't pretty. I wasn't anything. I had been made to feel worthless, but these beautiful people saw that I could learn." The Extension Service sent her to Costa Rica and Guatemala as an interpreter on a project to develop fish farms. She learned anatomy, chemistry, and the basic nutrition that she would teach to women in the community. Eva says that when she was on the cusp of entering the professional world, she was the "ugly gray" caterpillar that precedes the emergent butterfly. Breaking through her chrysalis "was my very first step out of a dark shell."

But *la mula* had trouble sticking to the rules. She was supposed to go only to women's homes to teach them about food groups. The food pyramid was her downfall. "How could I teach you nutrition if you had *no food*?" she asks. "How could I show you all these beautiful pictures in the pyramid of what you should eat? You know what you should eat, only the pocketbook doesn't know it." Eva began taking women to the local Safeway store to help them read labels and compare brands, teaching them savvy shopping. "Then I got caught. That wasn't my job." But Eva didn't get fired. She backed down and learned other ways to bend the rules. She helped women with whatever needs arose because, "you cannot teach a homemaker when she is being beat up or degraded in her own home. You have to build up to where she is. She can't think about nutrition for the body when she is depleted in the soul."

Though Eva speaks proudly of her entry into a professional world, she surveys her years in the fields with another kind of satisfaction. "I would take the kids out just so they would learn to pick onions after school. Or during the summer when they're not in school. I wanted them to do whatever jobs there are so that they would know, so that they would have everything." "Everything" includes remembering where they came from, even as Chayo moved to a position as a Head Start teaching assistant, Chana to a bank, Cami to health care, Maria to health and social services, and all of Eva's sons to various positions at the Amalgamated Sugar Company, including supervisory roles.

Eva praises all her children and the path each has chosen. She lauds their successes, even though they don't have the diploma. She still struggles with what might have been, and anger at the Nyssa schools lingers. But she acknowledges change and remains committed to creating opportunities for all the children in her community. She says, "You know, we can make people prisoners of a situation forever and that's not right. They can change and we can help them." For Eva, change depends on reaching back into the past for traditional practices as well as toward the future. Healing the lives of children in Nyssa depends as much on the roots of culture as it does on formal education.

16

Reviving the Root

La Enfermedad: We're struggling with young people
not going to school. We have snatched away their
language. We have made them feel like it's worthless.
This is why our branches are sick, because the
roots are sick. Their sap is not there anymore.

El Remedio: We need to speak Spanish, to use
our foods, our singing, whatever comes with
us. Be yourself. This is who you are. Never
leave the root. When we weave a basket, I
say, "This is how you weave your life."

"MIRA." Eva points at a clothesline of yellow, red, and pink
papel picado strung above our heads. Making cut paper, she notes,
proved a better use of Manuel's knife than his previous activities
as a gang member. In this aluminum-sided trailer at the edge of
Nyssa, Eva runs an arts program called Youth on the Move. Many
who come here trust no one but Eva, whom they call "Ipa," grand-

mother. Their creations fill the room. Drawings by two brothers who were kicked out of school for concocting a bomb line one wall. Multihued papier-mâché fish hang from the ceiling. Painted devils, traditional clay figures, and grinning animal masks line another wall. Day of the Dead altars adorn a table. Green and gold shards of colored glass shimmer into a flower on the surface of a table. Like many of Eva's art materials, the glass came from the city dump—like these kids, abandoned then salvaged.

This is work of the heart, Eva says. "My heart beat before I could speak. This is where it begins." Gang members regularly join young people who simply need a place to go; their parents labor in the fields or at the Amalgamated Sugar Factory across the street. Eva's focus is youth, but she reaches out to the family, as she does in her role as a *curandera*. Youth on the Move is now more than a decade old. Begun in 1993, it is the most recent version of programs that stretch back thirty years.

The first was Los Ecos de Cristo (The Echoes of Christ). Eva worked with more than sixty children, including her nine and their friends. The young people held the positions of secretary and treasurer. "The kids wanted to meet every day," she says, "but I was a wife and a mother. I had a job. We met once or twice a week at our house to read books." Meeting at Eva's kept them close to the huge locust tree—her dominant metaphor for keeping alive the traditions she hopes will sustain these kids. Those who cluster around the tree know their Ipa's dictum: "When the root is ruined, the limbs are sick, like our heritage that has been stripped and bitten away."

Many of Nyssa's youth come from migrant families, often indigenous. Eva's heritage gives her particular affinity for these groups. She laments that some children don't want to carry on indigenous languages. "These kids call them 'dinosaurs'; they don't think they need to know traditions," she says, "but someday they will." Eva tells young people, "Be yourself. This is who you are. Never leave the root. Because once you do, you start to die to yourself. Otherwise, God would have made us all the same. He wanted me to be a Mexicana and to look how I look." Cultural knowledge is the sustenance beyond bread that fed Eva as a child. "We had nothing and still I was a happy child. That's why I want to give this to these children." Traditional Mexican stories and arts can, she believes, heal dislocation and despair—the deep wounds of the spirit. "When we weave a basket, I say, 'This is how you weave your life.' They listen! They listen and I know it will be written in their hearts."

Once, when I referred to Eva as the program's director, she said, "I don't like that word. They direct me." She says of her mission, "It's just about love. I show respect for each one of them as they come in the door." The kids, in turn, must honor one another. "We misuse a lot of words. 'Love' and 'sex' are so abused. When teenagers use the four-letter word, I say, 'What's wrong with that? It's beautiful to do that. So when somebody uses that word and thinks it's harming you, laugh and say, 'Go ahead. I like it!' See if he ever says it again."

I gaze at the *papel picado* fluttering overhead, thinking of the past violence committed with the knife that cut that paper. Gangs have figured in eastern Oregon life for many years. Nyssa appears on a national list of places reporting the presence of gangs as early as 1970. But they've grown more active and visible. The Nyssa School District now forbids gang clothing and other symbols, as well as activities that solicit members. Penalties range from warnings to expulsion. The police department holds town meetings to help people identify gangs, their graffiti and paraphernalia, and to learn ways to combat them.

For Eva, the problem is not the gangs themselves, for what are they other than people seeking connection? They join, Eva says, because they feel "they belong together. They understand one another. Some don't have family, or the parents work too much." Kids need to form bonds to family, to community, to place. "The parents are not there. They want the new car. Everyone wants to get ahead." Eva sees this materialism and the individual striving celebrated in American culture as major culprits. Tradition offers at least a partial antidote. "We're struggling with young people not going to school. We have snatched away their language. We have made them feel like it's worthless. We need to speak Spanish, to use our foods, our singing, whatever comes with us."

Many sociologists locate the causes for gang membership in the same places Eva does: the need for ethnic and group identity, survival in a world where they feel marginalized, and escape from the problems of low-income neighborhoods and families. Yet gangs vary a great deal according to ethnicity, location, gender, and other factors.[1] Some groups that outsiders view as gangs see themselves as "street organizations." Noteworthy is the ALKQN (Almighty Latin King and Queen Nation) a collective that originated in Chicago and is now central to New York street life. Their internal structure of assemblies, rituals, dress, and gestures mimics that of a gang. But members of "The Nation" fast twice a month for cleansing; liberation theology informs their personal and social transformation. Luis Barrios, a social scientist and Episcopal priest, sees the spirituality harnessed by the ALKQN as a form of popular cultural religion and "an intrinsic component of all human beings."[2]

"They always say we're the gang," says one Almighty Queen. "But I'm not a gang member. I'm in an organization . . . I'm a mother trying to raise my kids right and tryin' to help others."[3] Any serious discussion of gangs must address how members define themselves as well as how outsiders view them. Activist Tom Hayden speaks to the broad demonization of such groups. "No one is more vilified today than a 'gang member,' with the exception of an 'international terrorist' or a 'narco-terrorist' . . . these shadowy personas are increasingly morphed into a single arch-enemy of society. The mainstream perception of order and well-being depends on the projection of an opposite, the barbarian."[4]

At a long table in the trailer, Eva and I flip through scrapbooks filled with photos of her young protégés. I need to report back to some of Eva's funding sources on program developments. Different organizations have granted money to her projects over the years: the Mexican-American Citizens League (MACL), the Rene Bloch Foundation, the Oregon Arts Commission, the Oregon Folk Arts Program, and the Eastern Oregon Regional Arts Council. But many of Eva's thirty years of work with kids was gratis. For a time, she incorporated these programs into her pursuit of a certificate in youth ministry. Illness thwarted that path, but Eva also realized that the certificate would just affirm what she was already doing. "I don't need money," she says. "I can be a minister by God. The gifts still come. I don't need their paper; their knowledge did help me. But it said to me, 'You're doing what is written here without knowing it.'"

Eva sometimes grows frustrated with agencies' expectations. "They want measurements and statistics, but how do you measure the child's first words after silence?" She points to a chair. "There was a young woman, fifteen years old, who sat there for weeks, saying nothing. Then, one day, a whisper, 'My daddy does things to me at night.' It was so hard for her to say. But she could come here day after day, just to sit, to wait. And you must wait with them. How do you know when a child will come to life?" Then, Eva's refrain that I have heard many times: "How do you measure faith? How much does it weigh? Can you say 'yesterday, I had ten pounds, today I only have one'?"

I wonder if recent events have strained Eva's faith. It's August 2003, just three months after the murder of her granddaughter Angie. When I woke early this morning in the casita, Eva had her back to me, staring out the window toward the Snake River. Sadness and anger filled her voice. "I have lions, Jo," she said. "I tie them back at night." The trial of Angie's husband, Abel, set for October, has been delayed. Eva worries that time will diffuse community outrage. Abel's defense lawyers claim they must go to Mexico to research his early life. "To show his adjustment problems," Eva says with disdain. She points to the "adjustment" problems her own family endured without complaint. How could the lawyers, she asks, use Mexican life, the very source of her strength, the core of her teachings to these kids, to excuse a violent murder? Recently, Eva walked with a group to the Nampa cemetery in commemoration, one of many efforts to keep Angie alive in our collective memory. She wants Abel brought to justice now but she dreads the trial. The prosecutor has warned the family not to cry out when they see the autopsy photos of the bullet's trajectory to Angie's heart. "Even if I'd seen it a thousand times, how could I not cry out?"

The creators of the papier-mâché fish and Day of the Dead altars in Eva's trailer have committed crimes—perhaps not murder, but other acts of violence. Yet, Eva does not transfer her anger at Abel and the legal system to them. She envisions young people differently, and she urges that altered vision onto us. "I tell you, Jo, from the bottom of my heart, I have never seen the people that the school describes, or the police. I have never seen it. And I have had them together here, the Blues and the Reds [rival gangs]."

Here is a story: One autumn, Eva was painting a mural on River Street in Ontario with a group from the Blues gang. She wanted to finish before the cold weather set in. When a car full of kids arrived and unloaded five-gallon paint cans, Eva thought, "Oh boy, we're going to get more help. It didn't cross my mind that something was wrong maybe because my heart is not that way." The boys poured the paint into pans, into which they dipped their long rollers. That's when Eva noticed red bandanas hanging from their back pockets—red that matched the paint they proceeded to roll over what Eva and the Blues had already sketched. "Trino Bravo was there," Eva says, pointing to a picture in the photo album of a boy standing near the corner of the mural. "Look at how red his face is; he was just mad! But he said to the other ones, 'Let's go. We're not gonna fight. Our Ipa is here.'"

Here is another story of how Eva's faith triumphed: She had the Blues and the Reds assembled at the trailer. A friend, Dave Jensen, called her from a special event at an Ontario hotel. They had abundant leftovers. Could she come to pick up the food? Eva promised to call Dave back and then asked the group, "Can you stay here together? Or can some of you go home?" She tested them with, "Do I need to buy pampers and bottles? What's gonna happen here if I leave?"

They yelled back in unison, "Nothing will happen!"

"On your word of honor?"

"On our word of honor."

Eva took five people with her to pick up the leftovers and returned to a calm and celebratory gathering. "We had all that wonderful food for a week."

Eva also teaches responsibility for one's actions. One day at the trailer, she urged a group of energetic boys to pound nails into blocks of wood. "Then they pulled out the nails," Eva says. "I said to them, 'See the holes that remain? You did that. Those don't go away.' They need to see what is left behind, the results of what they do." Sometimes those results cross the line for Eva. A young man who had helped her rebuild her house was among those she counted as her "angels." One day, she saw his wife with a bruised face and black eye. The verdict was "angel no more."

Over the years, with funding or her own money, Eva has traveled with young people to museums in Portland and Boise, to arts and cultural events, to schools and lectures. "We draw, we paint, we dance," she says of their adventures in Nyssa and beyond. Her devotion and spending sometimes irked her husband. "My Ted says that is why we don't have anything. I say we do. There are treasures all over. These kids are treasures. I tell you, they're golden." She points to some of the young people now grown to responsible adulthood, saying, "Here is Chanita. She's an artist. Here is Diego. He's a father a few times now." She can laugh, too, at the less dangerous foibles. "Oh, and here's the drunk," she says, remembering the Christmas pageant in which the Virgin Mary turned up reeking of liquor. "I was embarrassed from the top of my head to the bottom of my feet."

Some argue that young Latino gang members treat older women, the embodiment of motherhood, with greater respect. But beyond her status as a mother, grandmother, and healer, Eva has a special relationship to these young people because she accepts them. She points to a photo of a painting of women in black. "These are done by gang members. They admit it. That's who they are. " Her acceptance has prompted changes. She taps her finger on the painting to reinforce her point, "Look at the revolutionary women. They don't have guns and bullets. Those are roses across their chests." Other changes are small but significant. "I met one of the young men sometime after Halloween. He said, 'Ipa, I didn't do anything wrong on Halloween. I didn't do what I used to do because I remembered your words.'" Sadly, not everyone listened to Eva's words. Here are photos of Jesús and Felipe, now in jail.

Nor does everyone outside the Latino community listen. Eva recounts with chagrin the year that she took some gang members to Portland to create a Day of the Dead altar. "We had gathered the bread and the fruit and all the stuff, you know, for the altar." The manager of the Red Lion Inn refused to let the group use the restaurant or the hotel. "The man comes and says, 'Lady, I cannot have you with these young people here because my customers will not stop.'" Eva turned angry. The kids were hungry. But one young man offered the solution: "Ipa, don't worry. We'll eat the offerings to the dead!" Eva laughs as she tells this story, but the humor cloaks a determined goal: to overturn the narrative of Latino youth as violent and beyond reform. We change in part through the stories we tell one another about who we are—the balm for healing community schisms.

Eva's sympathy for the gang members deepened after Toe's death. At his funeral, dozens of young men and women that Eva had never met streamed in. As they walked past the casket, one by one, they pulled off the blue handkerchiefs worn across their chests and threw them into the casket. Eva watched, but only later did she fully realize that her Toe was likely a gang member. When

17

Healing Women

La Enfermedad: All the hurts! I thought
sometimes that I was the only one in the
world and that God put everything on me.

El Remedio: I would not change anything. Any
woman who comes into my path and touches
my life, I share that pain. Maybe she will not
have to go though all that. I can tell her, "Come
this way. It's not true that you have to do this or
that just to accommodate somebody else."

"CÓMO NO," Eva responds to the nurse from a local clinic who
has called with questions. Clinic workers are baffled by a frequently encountered phenomenon: young Mexicana and indigenous women wearing safety pins or keys hung in their bras. Eva
explains, "The mother is always scared that if there is an eclipse,
the moon is going to eat part of her child. If you have a chain of
safety pins or a key on you, then the moon cannot come and bite

your child. You'll have a whole child." Eva doesn't know the exact source of the belief. "It's a myth, a story. Something might have happened in our ancestry, so it's carried on." Part of Eva's strength as a healer is her discerning eye. Maintain the traditions that sustain people or are harmless, she argues; discard those that hamper growth. The safety pin may ease the gnawing dislocation immigrants feel. "I used to carry my key," she says. "I used to carry my safety pins so nobody would see them, but I had them. If I didn't, if my children had been maimed, I would have blamed myself for not having them."

Eva remembers her own entry to life in Pharr, Texas, and then in Nyssa. Familiar foods and symbols soothed her: garlic to guard against illness and *mal de ojo*; aloe vera or *siempre viva* (always alive)—the plant that "eats up everything negative in your house"; herbs and spices of the Mexican palate. "The *nopales* [cactus] are so good—cheap and very nutritious." Eva prizes her mother's *molcajete* for grinding spices and her *metate* as symbols of her heritage and of her parents' endurance in creating new lives. Similar objects and beliefs strengthen many Mexican women. Sometimes, however, traditional ways don't suffice.

On a clear spring night, a woman in jeans, black patent leather heels, and a light blue wool cardigan enters Eva's backyard, making her way past the koi pond. Eva waits with a group of other women. She offers a candle to the new arrival, who in turn offers the flame to the next person. The circle grows until the yard is radiant. Soft music plays from a boom box in the casita. Before coming here tonight, each woman received a handmade invitation with an open eye painted on a brightly colored door. Each has trouble she wants to shed; each hopes that an unburdening will happen here.

Any of the women might break from the circle to sit before an altar at the center and tell her story. On a pillow and soft blanket, "she births," Eva says. "Because to me, talking about those things is like birthing. It hurts. But if I birth it enough, if I go through the pain, one of these days it won't hurt anymore. It will be out."

From Eva's casita, I can see the koi pond and imagine this ritual. Surrounding us are the symbols of Mexican life in America: tiny clay pots and icons, the Virgin of Guadalupe hanging directly over the home altar. But Eva's altars also display figures of goddesses from various religions, and other symbols of women's power. The birthing ritual and similar practices are not traditions carried from Mexico and revived; Eva invents them to meet changing needs. "So many of us are wounded," Eva says. "If I have an accident out there on the road, you'll call the ambulance. But a lot of us are wounded in the spirit. Nobody sees it and we go on bleeding." Women, especially, need care for their social, spiritual, and psychological as well as physical well-being. "I see a lot of women," Eva says. "They're at home or working but they have no power. You're like a maid. 'Give me a dollar for a coke tomorrow.' But even if you don't work, he should give you money. He can go anywhere but you can't. Nobody empowers; at the church, they made us believe a lot of things I don't think are right. Well, no more!"

Eva's *testimonio* and crusade on behalf of women spring from her personal experience. "Where another woman ends, I start. Where I end, somebody else starts." She often treats women with suppressed menstruation and other conditions she sees as physical manifestations of psychic pain. "People are loveable and want to be touched. So I try to pass a little current of love to them. When we start talking, I find out that a lot of these women don't like sex because they feel used. They have never been kissed or touched in an erotic way. I think that has a lot to do with the ailments of people. I get X-rated! I am embarrassed, too, I get all hot and cold but I tell them." Once a new tradition is created, Eva argues, change begins. "If nobody talks about it, things will go on forever. How your mother lives, that's how you live, so will your daughters and so it goes."

Once, a *comadre* of Eva's called her to describe a backless dress she'd worn out dancing. "Eva, it buttons up at the neck, but there is nothing else," her friend confessed with relish. When she died a few years later, the woman's daughters asked Eva to help dress their mother for the funeral. "I don't know if I can without breaking down," Eva said, overwhelmed by the loss. "But I can help you select the clothes." They combed the closet and discovered the backless dress. "We would have to put a slip under that," said one daughter. Eva bit her tongue. Then they picked out toe rings and ankle bracelets from the jewelry box—baubles her daughters had never seen her wear. "When we lived in Texas, " Eva said, "we had to wear black and white—long black skirts and white blouses. Why shouldn't we wear colored dresses? Why did she have to hide these things from her daughters?" Older women especially, Eva argues, need freedom. "They said 'be obedient'—to husbands, the church—I say we need to be obedient to ourselves."

La mula's resistant spirit helps her to envision new customs. "We do beautiful things that we're not used to doing," she says of her invented ceremonies. "We meditate. I buy paper plates and candles. I put water in my little pond and float roses there—things that touch the heart and make it tender so that you can birth a lot of things that are going on inside of you for years." During these rites, Eva binds a group together symbolically, giving each person a small piece of string. "I hand my long piece to Cabella,

who was my helper; she ties her piece and hands the two strings
to the next. By the end of the circle, we're all together. No one
can take a piece of us. If we stick together, we're power. We're a
light to each other."

In the back of the casita, next to Eva's home altar, stand shelves of
her collections: muffin tins and antique kitchen implements she's
found at the bon marché; rows of flowered tea cups and saucers;
and her father's cutting board, worn smooth over nearly a hundred years of use. To one side leans an old silver coffee pot, the
kind used in formal hotel settings. Her sister Gorda gave her the
pot years before. "She got it at the bon marché and it was blacker
than black," Eva describes. "Gorda just threw it right there, saying, 'I brought you this because you're always picking up ugly
things.'" At that time, Eva was in love with another man, though
she remained married to Ted. She suffered tremendous guilt. "A
woman, when this happens to her, she's a bad woman, but see,
I'm not a bad woman. I was all mixed up, and it was very, very
traumatic for me. I would pray on my hands and knees. And I
would hear this voice, always behind my left shoulder. I would
hear it. I am not dreaming; I am not *loca*. I hear things. When I
would pray the Our Father, I would put out my hands so he could
put things in."

Soon after Gorda gave her the pot, Eva received a number of
requests to visit women's groups. One day, an invitation came to
address a gathering of sixty women. Eva hesitated. "What am I
going to say? I'm bad. I'm in love with a man who's not my husband." As she pondered a response, she arranged flowers in the
tarnished coffee pot. "I got Ajax and the washrag and started
working on that pot. And I'll be darned if it wasn't shinier than

shiny. Just brilliant and beautiful! That gave me the idea of what I would say. We get dirty or they get us dirty—the rest. But we are silver or gold. We're thought of as ugly like that pot, but anybody who takes the time to believe in what I have to say will help me shine. So, this is what I'm going to tell them." Eva spoke to the group. As a finale, she tore up a clean diaper into small pieces. She distributed the pieces of cloth, instructing the women to shine the symbolic blackened pots of their lives—their own spirits when others failed to believe in them.

The results astonished Eva. Vans full of women arrived at her house. To Eva's chagrin, they believed the magic was embedded in the cloth. Everyone had a story: the cloth had saved her from jail or brought lottery money. Eva argued, "It's not the cloth. It's faith." The women had misinterpreted her use of symbols, transferring power to an object. She began to doubt her path as a healer. "I would pray at my altar and say, 'Lord, you give me a sign that what I am doing is good. I feel so terrible about this.' I would take this awful feeling and put it in a bag and give it to God and say, 'I don't want it. Take it, keep it.' He would throw it right back at me. I haven't been able to escape. He gives me everything I ask now because I have taken it in with all my heart, all my suffering, and he won't take it back. He wants me to have it."

One frigid morning not long after the coffee pot incident, Eva went out back to gather kindling for the fire. "There was a lot of snow. I started out, and I felt these hands turn my head around and heard a voice saying, '*Mira.*' And there in the snow, there was this long hole. I looked straight in and there's this little face. I scratched the snow and got hot water to pry it out. It was just a little stick but it felt like a person. I took it in my arms and carried it in and sat on the sofa. I was crying for happiness, for a lot of emotions that I have never felt before, but I was also listening. It was just like a person, that stick, talking to me about not being afraid."

At first, Eva didn't tell anyone this story. Sometimes she doubted her own experience; she tried showing the stick to others. No one considered it special. But Eva had spent many years seeing what others don't see; hearing voices others don't hear; healing through magical thinking; "pretending" she doesn't have the disease she will not name and keeping the door closed to the "Big C—the big fat woman who knocks." She had spent years watching women ascend to heights others decreed impossible. Eva finally embraced the stick and its message. The path of helping others, especially women, would remain her work. "This is what I needed," she declares. "I asked for proof, he gave it to me. He even talked to me." The stick still rests on her altar to assure her and to aid in healing. But even if the stick disappeared, Eva would honor its power. The things of the world may burn to the ground, but symbols endure. The stick beckoned, she says, so that "I wouldn't be afraid to be who I am and to do what I have to do in the situations that come to me every day."

"*Basta*!" Eva says as she raises her hands chest high and pushes outward in resistance. "Enough!" Since Angie's murder, Eva has marched to and from the Nampa cemetery, attended rallies to end domestic violence, and witnessed Abel Leon's sentencing to life imprisonment. The presiding judge said, "I do find, Mr. Leon, that you so utterly lack rehabilitative potential that imprisonment until death is the only feasible means of protecting society."[1] Even at the end, Leon took no responsibility for the crime. He pleaded guilty to first-degree murder by using an Alford plea, which merely acknowledges that prosecutors could likely prove the charges against him.

From the back room of her casita, Eva brings out an oblong carrying case. Inside are objects she created for a Nampa art exhibit intended to draw attention to violence against women. Eva pulls out a black box about six inches wide and two feet in length, narrower at one end. The miniature casket houses Eva's hand-dipped wax flowers—the same creations that carry a young woman into adulthood at her *quinceañera*, that crown her hair and link her to a husband with the wedding *lazo*. But unlike the glistening whites, pinks, and spring greens of those *coronas*, these flowers are black and blue. "The color of bruises," Eva explains. She fears that the organizers of the exhibit won't want her caskets. "I haven't heard from them. Maybe I'm too intense," she shrugs. Then, she looks up to the hand-crocheted Virgin of Guadalupe, her head bent toward us, hands joined in prayer. Eva's face softens. Then *la mula* resurfaces. "La Virgen will be in the exhibit, too, but her hands won't be folded in prayer. No more!" Eva flips open her palms to illustrate her vision for the Virgin. "Her hands will be stretched out. She's saying, 'I'm ready to work. What will it take?'"

18

A Courageous Heart

La Enfermedad: I didn't raise my sons to kill, but I did raise them to be free and to help others be free.

El Remedio: Before he left for Iraq, I told my son, "I gave you a courageous heart but not a stupid one."

WHEN I CALLED EVA IN JULY 2004, her voice broke on the phone. "How can I say this, Jo? I don't want people to ask me how I am." Her grandson Kenny, Maria's son, back a month from Iraq, had signed up for another tour of duty. How could he not return, Kenny asked Eva, when he saw how poor the people are? Then her son Marty's National Guard unit was called. With his nineteen-year-old nephew about to depart, wouldn't it be shameful for him to refuse? He has a responsibility to the Guard, Eva said on the phone, but he also has children and a wife and duties here. Eva's unresolved feelings emerged as we spoke; resistance and national pride fought each other for dominance.

I could almost hear her father's voice in her ear: "I'd rather be a

poor man in America than a millionaire in Mexico." Patriotism,
hard work, and honesty form the foundational pyramid of Fidel
Silva's dream. He railed against collecting welfare, called for self-
sufficiency, and pledged when he became a permanent resident
never to be a burden to the U.S. government. These beliefs filtered
into Eva's life and her children's. Such sentiments feel as American
as the red, white, and blue cup holder Eva's grandson J.R. gave me
when we visited Chayo and Ricardo's in Texas, the one that reads
"Proud to be an American/United We Stand." They feel as American as the yellow ribbons that adorned Eva's wrought-iron fence
one day on a previous visit. Kenny was due home from his first
tour then. I remember feeling dizzy, not knowing what was different about the house, until the yellow ribbons came into focus. But
something else had always left me disoriented when Eva talked
about war and about being Mexican and American. Later, she
would tell me about a conversation with Marty before he left for
Iraq. "I said to him, 'I gave you a courageous heart but not a stupid one.'" As is sometimes the case, I couldn't discern Eva's exact
meaning. Her statement seemed open to so many interpretations.

Perhaps that's because the Latino involvement in American
wars, from the Revolution to Iraq, has been complex and contradictory. Latinos and other minorities are often overrepresented
based on their percentage of the United States population. This
came to the fore during the war in Vietnam, which sharply divided
the Latino community. The rate of enlistment remained high, but
Vietnam also brought together Chicano and antiwar activists.
This duality of patriotism and resistance continues. A high percentage of immigrants and long-settled Mexican Americans fight
for this country while others oppose entry into a system that continues to discriminate. A 1991 report by the National Council of

La Raza points to a long-standing pattern of Latinos in the military as "disproportionately concentrated in the lowest pay grades, with the lowest level of responsibilities and fewest opportunities."[1] Jorge Mariscal argues that the armed forces illuminate "the contradictions at the heart of U.S. society's treatment of its own citizens of Mexican descent."[2] Why die for a country that treats you like a second-class citizen?

While Marty, Kenny, and many others Mexican Americans served in Iraq, others argued against the war from its inception. By December 2006, a report by the Pew Hispanic Center documented Hispanics' growing disapproval of the war in Iraq. When asked how they thought the military effort was going, 68 percent of Hispanics responded, "not well at all." Further, two-thirds of Hispanics, compared with half of the overall U.S. population, favored bringing the troops home from Iraq "as soon as possible."[3]

In August 2006, my husband, Bob, and I drive across the state to visit Eva. Marty returned from Iraq nearly six months before. He and Eva planned to come to Portland the previous May. Marty was to receive a medal of honor for his duty in Iraq; his best friend from nearby Ontario would be granted the same award posthumously. He had died in Marty's arms, a fact Eva reported over the phone with a quiver in her voice. They never made it to Portland for the ceremony. Eva didn't say why; I suspected they feared triggering the trauma. Marty had spoken little of war's lingering effects. Now, whatever other fears for her son hover under the surface, Eva's overwhelming sentiment is gratitude, "We have our Marty back."

Bob and I lounge on an overstuffed green couch in the casita when Marty arrives. He sits across from us, which gives him a full view of the gallery of heroes on the wall—Eva's sons in uniform. All have served in the National Guard, though only Marty has been called to war. I haven't seen him for several years. His angular, handsome face has thinned. His hairline is receding a bit now, evident when he takes off the baseball cap emblazoned with "One nation under God" and an American flag.

Like all Eva's children, Marty is polite and personable. As he warms up, stories emerge of his life in Iraq as Sergeant C. "They couldn't say 'Castellanoz'?" I ask, incredulous. Marty just grins. This amiable manner and his competence at multiple kinds of work propelled him from a position as a cook at a Texas base to sergeant in charge of a unit near Kirkuk. His story alternates between frustration at the futility of the mission—"They [the Iraqis] are never going to be ready to take charge"—and appreciation for the abundance of life in the United States—"We have no idea of hard lives." He describes how people drink, bathe, wash clothes, and urinate in the same river. He tells of children who broke his heart. He would walk the streets of the villages distributing sweets from his care packages. One young boy always stood apart. When Marty discovered that he was an Arab in a predominantly Kurdish community, he watched out for him. One day, Marty received a package with children's clothing, including a pink Barbie shirt. He didn't see the little boy on his next trip to the village, so he found out where he lived. When Marty knocked on the door, a man answered. Behind him, everyone hit the floor. "They were so afraid," Marty says, chagrined. He beckoned to the little boy and gave him the shirt. "After that, I never saw him without it."

As Marty finishes, I fight tears. I'm grateful when his wife, Priscilla, arrives, and we distract ourselves by explaining to Bob why she is called "Flaca" for her skinny frame. I keep my emotions in check as we move onto other topics. But for days afterward, I return to this story, hovering between despair and gratitude that human beings can summon their best selves under the worst circumstances.

In May of the following year, I talk to Eva just after she's returned from a trip with Marty to the veterans' hospital in Boise. Out front, a sign reads, "The price of war is seen here." "These are just words," Eva says, "until you see the people inside. Then you know that they are not lying." Marty discourages Eva from attending his meetings; he needs to talk about things that he doesn't want his mother to hear. Despite all the trauma Eva has endured and helped others through as a healer, she has no experience with ordeals of this kind. "I haven't seen dead people in piles on the road, with dogs eating them." Eva tries not to eavesdrop but sometimes the temptation is too great. She cannot repeat what she hears. Instead, she tells me about earlier wounds Marty suffered.

When he was about thirteen, Marty got caught between the tractor and the potato harvester when he was in the fields with Ted. They waited hours for an ambulance. They feared that gangrene would set it and his leg would have to be amputated. But Marty recovered, his leg intact. "He's been through so much," Eva says. "He is strong." She points with pride to his years as a five-state boxing champion. He and his brother Ralph have both accumulated numerous boxing trophies. At times Eva would recoil when watching them fight, especially Marty. "I didn't want to see him beat up. I didn't want to see him beat up other people. But he was good!" These days, Eva looks at her son's handsome face in her photo gallery to "give her power." "Right now," she says, "I'm looking at my Marty and his son, who looks just like my dad." As she speaks, I see the direct line from Fidel Silva through his grandsons, and I wonder what his patriotism—one leg of his foundational dream of life in America—means to Eva now.

Eva repeats, "We have our Marty back," adding, "at least his body." He sleepwalks at night, sometimes going into town. One Nyssa police officer is a friend of Marty's, who also served in Iraq. He understands; he brings Marty home. Disability payments will help financially. This is important because yesterday, Marty forgot to go to his job at the Amalgamated Sugar plant in Nampa where Ricky and Ralph also work.

Nearly two years after Marty returned from Iraq, Eva calls to relate a story that shows her son is "really back." "Jo," she says with excitement, "he is doing a new program with kids called MC." The initials stand for both "Martin Castellanoz" and "Makers of Champions." In teaching young men to box, Eva tells me, he is actually helping to shape "Champions in Life." Traditional arts are Eva's tools for teaching personal and social transformation; boxing is Marty's. He guides people toward social responsibility as they hone their skills. I remember how animated he grew that day in Eva's casita when he described the young boy in the Barbie shirt. Now, I imagine that vitality reemerging to aid Nyssa's youth.

As I hang up from our phone call, I recall my conversation with Eva the day she told me about her fears for Marty and Kenny in Iraq. Before she described their decision to enlist, I had asked how she planned to spend her day. "Chana just got here," she said. "We're pulling weeds. I talk to them when I pull, 'I'm sorry that you have to go but you're choking my cucumbers!' They just want to live, too. We all just want to live."

19

How Not to Be

La Enfermedad: I drove up to Washington and got
off on the wrong road. When I stopped to ask
some boys for directions, they told me how to
go. Then one of them said, "Yeah, this time to get
there, you won't have to swim across the river."

El Remedio: When they said that to me, I looked
right at them and said, "Thank you very much.
You have showed me how not to be."

ON A FEBRUARY DAY IN 2007, I pick Eva up at a hotel off
Barbur Boulevard in southwest Portland. She's come for a ceremony to honor Oregon's eight living National Heritage Award
winners. She loads my old Honda with coolers of tamales, homemade tortillas, beans, and rice that she brought for my husband,
Bob, and me. Chana, who drove from Nyssa, will remain at the
hotel with Eva's sick great-granddaughter, Tatiana. Eva worries
over the baby's illness and the fate of her car. It is once again in

the repair shop, having sputtered to a standstill soon after they arrived.

At the Oregon History Center, about forty people mill about the Madison Room. Award recipients range from ninety-three-year-old Hmong qeeg player Bua Xou Mua to Irish fiddler Kevin Burke to Native American bead artist and basket weaver Sophie George. The ceremony opens with each commenting on how the award changed his or her life. When Eva rises, she shows no signs of current worries or the mixed emotion that this honor triggers for her. In 1989, the call from Washington DC came one day after the car wreck that killed her son Toe. Eva speaks calmly, graying curls falling to her shoulders, head held high, stunning me as she always does with her eloquence.

In some ways, the award didn't alter Eva's life. She has always shared traditional arts with her community through projects like Youth on the Move. As part of the Oregon Folklife Program's Traditional Arts Apprenticeships, she taught her granddaughter Erika to make *coronas*. Family and community acknowledgment sufficed as reward. But national recognition catapulted Eva into the public eye. The geographic range of her teaching broadened; she traveled to New York and Washington DC for festivals. The award also launched her career as a community scholar. In the early 1990s, she documented Latino arts for the Oregon and Idaho Folk Arts programs, helping to develop exhibits and publications. She added photography and interviewing skills to those she had already developed.

Now, she traverses the Northwest to demonstrate traditional arts at festivals and in libraries and schools. The trunk of her car brims with crepe paper, pipe cleaners, wax, and her old wok. In teaching about Mexican culture, Eva incorporates a personal philosophy about "how to be" and "how not to be" in the world. Sometimes her message is implicit, occasionally more overt. The first time I saw her make *coronas* was at a 1990 festival in Idaho. She stood before a group of children and their parents and offered clear, simple instructions for living as well as for flower making:

> Pick any kind of paper. Bright Mexican crepe paper is best. But you can use old paper, even grocery bags—white or blue or yellow or brown. Save things that you might throw away. Ask yourself, "What's that good for?" Remember that the things or people that we think are the least—they are the most. Find the good, just like with people. I have my own special inner magnifying glass. Maybe there's this person that people say, "She's no good." Everybody puts her to the side. But I know there is a tiny dot of good in her, so I have to take out the magnifying glass and find it. It's there.
>
> Cut the crepe paper into four-inch pieces. You will need eight to ten pieces for each flower. Cut each piece into petals and curl into small, tight rolls. Wrap the stem with green tape, then dip the flower into wax at 120 degrees, shucking off the excess like a dog shaking off water at the beach. Bleach the outer edge with Clorox or alcohol to intensify the color at the center. This helps to make them more real. Remember that the flowers are alive. They have a voice and can speak. God made them perfect. We can't make them perfect but we can try.

The most spectacular results come from small children and troublesome teens. They might be overweight boys in baggy shorts and backward baseball caps, acting out and laughing. Until Eva begins to speak. She commands the room, capturing attention as if she were engaged directly with each individual. "If I make flowers for you," she says, "I look into your eyes and I see you, then I

pray and want all these good things for you. That's why they are
not for sale. I don't think that feeling and love can ever be bought."

On this February day, I watch how Eva draws people to her,
as though magnetized. After the awards ceremony, she sits at the
edge of the Madison Room. People line up near her chair. Though
Eva teaches through material arts, stories are an equally powerful
vehicle. When I step outside to call the repair shop about her car,
she begins to tell a friend an account I'd already heard. "There is
a young Mexican man," Eva describes a worker in the Salvation
Army store in Ontario. "They say he is 'slow.' The store manager yells at him when he makes mistakes. Last time, they were
yelling at him about giving me too many pennies. I just gave him
back a quarter and said, 'You are doing a really good job. Remember that.'" She waits for a moment, then adds, "Salvation Army?
Whose salvation are they talking about? All we can do is what we
know is right. To tell the truth. These bad things happen to you so
that you can know how it feels, then speak the truth."

Telling her truths can cause conflict for Eva, sometimes with
her own community. When she began doing fieldwork, some Latinos in Oregon challenged her willingness to share their traditions
with a broader public. "But how else will people understand one
another?" Eva asks. Her artistry and skill at translating between
cultures brought her to the attention of the Oregon Arts Commission. Nearly a decade after her National Endowment for the Arts
award, Eva was appointed to the state's commission—the first traditional artist to hold that post. She served from 1997 through
2001. Commission work posed challenges. At times, she was ill;
other times, she had to find childcare for grandchildren staying
with her in order to attend meetings. But Eva found deep fulfill-
ment in that work. She increased attention to traditional arts and

achieved one of her unchanging goals: to help others "see differently." For Eva, envisioning art in a new way locates its power at the fulcrum of daily life. Like healing, art connects to food and spirituality and other aspects of culture. *Coronas* and Day of the Dead altars may appear in museums, but they truly live in the community. These arts also speak to non-Latinos because the human impulse to create beauty is a force that unites us.

Eva's stories about "how to be" often involve "tying back the lions" of anger. Here is another story: a few weeks before the awards ceremony, she went shopping in Boise. "I love beautiful things," she says. "I have an expensive eye." As Eva parked in front of an exclusive home décor shop, the owner came out with a "reserved parking" sign. She looked at Eva's old car and motioned to the storefront next door—a payday loan company. Eva thought the woman was just confused. "No, I'm coming to your shop," she explained. The owner retreated. Inside, Eva pointed to a hand-woven basket on the wall. The owner shook her head, "That's very expensive." Eva's voice shook with emotion as she described the pivotal point at which she understood the woman's intent. Then she made her choice about "how to be." "I told her that I wanted that basket," Eva said. "When I left, I said I would be back. She will get to know me. I will help her to see." The same day of this encounter, Eva discovered that a young man she used to work with had been indicted for shooting another gang member. "I know he has a cruel heart," Eva said, "but I think about how anger builds up . . ." Her voice trailed off.

The frequent travel Eva's work requires imparts different kinds of lessons, as fear and other demons rise to the surface. In 2006, Eva drove to Leavenworth, Washington, to make *coronas* at the town's annual salmon festival. En route, she got off on the wrong road and panicked. "When I stopped to ask some boys for directions, they told me how to go. Then one of them said, 'Yeah, this time to get there, you won't have to swim across the river.'" Eva kept her voice calm. "When they said that to me, I looked right at them and said, 'Thank you very much. You have showed me how not to be.'" Later, she reported her delight in learning about the salmon's migration back to the streams of their birth. "It was so wonderful, Jo. The salmon, the way they find their way home! The sacrifice they make!" She might have been describing her own sometimes treacherous journeys home from teaching about traditional arts.

Earlier in 2007, she lost her oldest friend, Agapita. "She was my *comadre*," Eva mourned. They had met in Pharr when Eva married Ted. "I was fifteen and Agapita was nineteen," Eva said. "She saw everything that happened to me with Ted, my crazy life. She was my witness and now she's gone and I wonder, did all of that really happen?" Eva was determined to go to the funeral in Arizona. Though she often flies to Texas to see her children, air travel remains a trial. "I am not a big people person," Eva said of the crowds and claustrophobia she experiences in airports and on planes. "But I had to go to be with Agapita's daughters. They call me 'Madrina.' I wanted to be there for them." In the terminal, Eva grew nervous about missing her flight. Indifferent clerks sent her running between airlines until she nearly missed her plane. "My heart was racing," she said. "I vomited and then got a nosebleed." Everyone ignored her until an airline worker explained that the flight was delayed. "Why couldn't they have said that sooner?" Eva asked, exasperated. Was it racism? Harried workers? Old pain resurfaced from childhood—fear of *la migra*, panic at being in the wrong place at the wrong time.

When I return to the Madison Room with happy news about

the car, Eva smiles. She has been praying to San la Muerte. This recent addition to her pantheon of saints is better than travel insurance. A recent drive from a festival in Washington left her exhausted. She feared she wouldn't make it to her friend María's in Hermiston, just over the Oregon border. "I started talking to myself," Eva said, "and praying to San la Muerte. I said to Muertecito, 'Lend me your eyes.' And I started going straight on the road. I could see and I made it to María's." This experience got repeated a few weeks later. Again, San la Muerte helped her by saying, "Lift the dress from your eyes." Eva's hand swept upward, and she could see again. "We are human. Our hearts start beating fast," she says of her terror of getting lost or being forced off the road by a group of young men, as she almost was on a recent trip. "But I go anyway. I never travel alone. The Holy Spirit is with me." I remembered our trip to Texas, Eva at the Falfurrias checkpoint, Eva in the *milagro* room at the Basilica of Our Lady of San Juan del Valle. Faith as the opposite of fear.

Once, I asked Eva how she always arrives on time—a major feat given her problems with cars and penchant for getting lost. "I trust," she said of her fluid relationship to time. "We may plan. I may have a calendar and a plan—I'm amazed to see people planning through the year—but Mexicanos, *mañana*. No time. I hardly ever carry a watch. I walk, maybe the next step I will fall. But I trust I won't." One year, Eva was scheduled to visit my class, Gender in Cross-Cultural Perspective, at Lewis and Clark College. I knew she'd have to calculate carefully to cross Oregon and arrive by three in the afternoon. Trouble arose in Nyssa with some gang members in her Youth on the Move program. She didn't want to leave them so she borrowed a van. At exactly three, she walked in the door of the classroom with fifteen teenagers.

Families and friends of the National Heritage Award winners begin to drift from the Madison Room. We leave the Oregon History Center to retrieve Eva's car in northwest Portland before nightfall. Outside, fragrant hyacinths and tiny white pansies bloom in Portland's "false spring." But winter's shadow lingers. Eva hunches against the cold as we walk from the museum to my car. She wears a white fleece jacket over a red blouse and cotton pants, white anklets under brown two-inch heels. Her bon marché clothes look elegant, marked by Eva's signature sense of style. "Someone told me the other day that I should wear different clothes," she says when I note her outfit. In the car, Eva expands the story. When she returned to Nyssa after Agapita's funeral, she related her trials at the airport to a Mexican friend. The woman cast an eye on Eva's embroidered blouse. "If you dressed differently, people would treat you better," the friend remarked, advice Eva interpreted as "look less Mexican." As I turn onto I-5, Eva bursts forth with her ultimate testimonial of "how to be." "This is how I dress. This is who I am. I am the woman who scrubs your toilet. I am the woman who picks your corn. I am the woman who stands in the factory line. I'm here and I look this way. And I, too, am the image of God."

20

La Casa

La Enfermedad: In Nyssa, we started out living
with my parents. My sister was already married
and my little brothers had the living room.
Ted and I and our kids were in the bathroom—
a tiny four-by-something room where we had
to cover the bathtub and make our bed.

El Remedio: I was pregnant with Cami when I built
our house. They didn't think I could do it. But the
only time I took off was the three days I was in the
hospital. I was very pregnant, very skinny, but I had
the strength and I did it. It was such a wonderful
time, because the house was for my children.

DRIVING ACROSS OREGON in spring 2008, ryegrass cover
crop alternates with brown earth. Snow still gleams on the Blue
Mountains and the Boise range northeast of Nyssa in Idaho. Bob
and I follow the route markers I remember from my first trip to

Eva's nearly twenty years before: a left turn off Highway 201, straight past the Owyhee Beer Distributing Company, right on Third Street at the bright blue Rodriguez Bakery, several doors down to Eva's brick and wrought-iron fence. All feels familiar but the house. For the past five years, I've arrived to find the burned sheathing of Eva's home. Now the rebuilding is nearly complete. Plastic still covers the window frames. Light yellow siding blends with the young green of barely visible buds on the bushes outside. We park and approach the house for a closer look, drinking in the musky scent of new wood.

Without Eva's garden in full bloom, everything in the backyard stands out: Xochitl's beige and purple playhouse with her name, birthdate, and the address—2001 Love Street—engraved on the side; rusty buggy wheels that punctuate the iron fencing; cherubs and angels alongside a plaque that I suspect Eva found at the bon marché: "Dance as though no one is watching." Eva waits out back in the casita. She looks young and stylish in a cropped cotton top and khaki pants; her hair weaves in gray and black curls that fall to her neck. With every year I've known her, she has lost weight. Her beauty is angular now, but the softness that filled her eyes in the photo taken at age sixteen remains.

We sit and talk as Eva sautés nopales picked from her greenhouse next door. She extols cactus as a source of cheap protein. "They say we should eat organic now. My parents were so poor, what else could they eat? The best things are very simple." Eva rolls dough into thin tortillas with an expertise perfected over many years. She holds up her hands. "I got called for my biometrics," she says of a recent visit to the immigration office, "and they could not find my fingerprints." When I asked why they would call her, a longtime permanent resident, she just shrugged. "I told them that my fingers are worn. I have worked very hard for so many years. They said that I was dehydrated. Now I'm drinking water and putting on Corn Huskers Lotion." But with a grin Eva adds, "I don't think they're going to find my fingerprints."

We eat with relish, relaxing in the suddenly spacious casita. The purple and green swirl pattern on the linoleum floor reappeared when Eva moved her furniture into the rebuilt house. We're anxious for a tour, having monitored the house's slow rebirth. Friends in Boise and Portland, Nampa and Nyssa, held fundraisers after the fire. Old friends and strangers—all part of Eva's network of "angels"—came forward to help. One group is a women-owned rug company from Boise whose workers supplied and installed the carpet. Others helped with construction. Eva's children, their lives already full with family and jobs, contributed the most, toiling on weekends and at night.

When we visited the year before, mounds of thick pink insulation covered the floor. We'd arrived to find Maria and her husband, Rojelio, with staple guns, soon joined by Ricky, Ralph, Chana, and her husband, Brown, and a gaggle of their kids. Each had brought a dish for Sunday dinner—Mexican rice, beans, tortillas, and a specialty called "violated chicken"—a bird impaled on an open beer can and slow-cooked on the grill. We lingered, telling stories into the evening. Xochitl, then eight years old, played without her oxygen tank. A small pump worn on her chest in a cloth sack adorned with a smiling bear had replaced the tube extending from her nose. Maria, by necessity an authority on her daughter's condition, monitored the pump. At one point, a possible occlusion occurred. In a flash, Maria was on the phone to the Denver hospital where Xochitl has had twenty-one operations. "We've been blessed," she says of Xochitl's life. Chana and

Brown told of a recent encounter with the IRS. The agency mistakenly transposed numbers on their tax forms; letters flooded their mailbox demanding payment of $10,000 on the previous year's alleged salary of $104,000. Chana and her husband collapsed with laughter at the absurdity of such financial plenty. Despite Brown's two jobs and hers with the bank, they had no health insurance. Ralph, having endured the murder of his child, described the happy challenges of caring for Angie's kids. He legally adopted the three children, who live part time with him and part time with their grandmother Sylvia in Nampa. These family stories detail events that would turn many people bitter. Yet, Eva's children tell their tales without rancor, each story balm to a past wound.

Since the house burned down, Eva has rarely admitted to her own hardships. She confesses that winter chills the casita; I've heard her say many times, "I would rather be hungry than cold." Once, she told me that she wept when she pulled into her driveway at night and saw the blackened shell of her house. But mainly, she likens the house's resurrection to a birth, "We have to wait for a baby to be ready." Eva's gratitude to the community and her children runs deep. Still, she stunned me with a revelation during dinner. "I'm going to stay in the casita," she said. "The house will be for Ralph and Angie's kids." My initial shock quickly dissolved, for the house has always been about Eva's children.

On a visit over a decade before, I was staying with Eva when her youngest child, Cami, stopped over en route to work at the Malheur Memorial Health Center. He stands over six feet tall, but his gentle manner endeared him to the sick clients. "That man is the one they call for," Eva said of Cami's popularity. As he bid goodbye, Eva looked up with affection. "I was pregnant with Cami when I built this house. It was such a wonderful time because the house was for my children."

The government-sponsored project actually began when Eva was pregnant with her eighth child, Toe. The ten families selected would provide the sweat equity. Each had to commit to build and inhabit the house upon completion. Eva suspected she would not be approved because she worked in the fields. She had to convince Ted to sign the commitment papers, and then she battled to build outside the city limits. "I wanted space for my kids because they have never been town or city people." Finally, the project managers approved her request. On the first day, she joined the other families. "Nine men, plus their wives and some of the older kids all going out to work—and here was this woman," Eva said of herself. "Just her, with her old father sometimes. A pregnant woman. They didn't think I could do it. But 'the Bills'—both of the supervisors were named Bill—said, 'She works the whole day. She works more than we do!' The only time I took off was the three days I was in the hospital. I was very pregnant, very skinny, but I had the strength and I did it." Eva whispered to Toe in the womb, telling him he would be born in a new home. But the construction took over two years. It was Cami whose life began in the house with the Castellanoz plaque on the door.

Now, as we finish our tacos with nopales, Chayo calls from Texas. Eva passes the phone to me. I always welcome reconnection to this family who hosted me so generously on our trip to Pharr in 2001. Chayo describes her pursuit of a certificate to teach American Sign Language. Cami has moved to Texas to help Chayo care for her grandchildren, cook, and keep house. "They are all there for one another," Eva beams with pride as she hangs up.

We leave the casita for a tour of the new structure. Inside, the kitchen's beige tile and blond wood cabinets gleam. Neutral-colored carpet runs through the house. An overstuffed couch and comfortable reading chairs in red and white cotton print brighten the living room. A tiffany shade, a gift from Maria, suspends from the ceiling. On the front wall hangs a large flat clock with "Paris" written across its face, found on one of Chana's bargain hunts. Eva's daughters chose the bedrooms colors. The Guadalupe Room is light pink with one dark pink wall. In the bathroom, a lovely 1940s-style washbasin displays the fifty-dollar price tag. Pink towels marked $1.75 from the bon marché fill the linen closet. "There are treasures everywhere," Eva says of her gleeful bargain hunting.

Everything is clean, spare, and new. The house might be anywhere in America but for the spirits of Eva's "Mexicanidad," waiting to reinhabit their space: the clay pots that will reclaim the kitchen corner; the *metate* and *molcajete* waiting for counter space; the hangings of the Virgin of Guadalupe; the photo gallery of Eva's children, grandchildren, and great-grandchildren that "give power" to her each day.

We're still digesting lunch when the clan arrives with dinner. Loss of the house never slowed down the ritual Sunday meal. Another "violated chicken," beans, rice, salads, and tortillas are spread across the makeshift table of plywood over wooden sawhorses, a floral oilcloth on top. We sit on green plastic lawn chairs; Maria and Chana urge Bob and me to fill our plates first. I chat with Diego about his family and his work on the school board. Ralph surveys the progress on the house; he has decided to stay in his own home, Eva tells me, so that she can move back in. Marty has returned from a boxing match in Boise, where one of his young protégés won. As Ricky grills onions with Yolanda, I remember Eva's story of his dutiful dinner preparation each night when she

arrives home from work. Maria fills a plate for Xochitl, about
to turn ten and nearly as tall as her mother. Chana and Brown's
daughters are working at the Ontario Red Apple grocery, due to
graduate from high school. The family's IRS woes remain unsettled; Chana smiles as she tells the story.

The vroom of a sports car into the driveway disrupts the early
evening quiet. Eva looks surprised; she has discouraged Sunday
visitors. Though this is a traditional *limpia* day, Sunday is also
sacrosanct family time. But when a red-haired woman in a stylish leather coat emerges from the car, Eva waves in recognition.
She walks toward the casita, gesturing for Bob and me to follow.
Eva introduces Lydia, who agrees to let us witness her healing
session.

Eva sits at one end of the table, Lydia at the other. From a round
woven tortilla basket, Eva takes a deck of cards. She shuffles and
cuts, then spreads them out. "*Dame veinte* [Give me twenty]," she
says. Lydia chooses cards "with the eyes of her soul," Eva explains.
As she lays the cards out, Eva asks Lydia about the man who's been
living with her. Lydia suspects he's seeing younger women but she
doesn't want to kick him out. "You have a nice house," Eva says.
"You worked hard for that, what man wouldn't want to move in?
But can you trust him?" Lydia replies that she needs help with fix-
ing things. Just recently, the fan broke. "You can't hire someone?"
Eva's voice rises with incredulity. She points to the cards, one long
fingernail drumming a queen of hearts. "*Mira*. Look inside to find
what you need." Self-sufficiency and community are both essential
to healing. After another half hour of talking, Lydia thanks Eva,
leaving a few dollars as she hugs her goodbye. Eva verbalizes no
judgment on Lydia's situation. But as we rejoin the dinner gathering, she nods toward the reincarnated building, "I built that house

myself. I dug this foundation. I made all the trusses." She does not
need to remind us: she did it alone.

Eva's sons have now drifted to the west side of the table, daughters to the east. Diego starts to taunt Maria. From his position on
the city council, he says, he intends to introduce an ordinance that
women must make homemade tortillas. Chana and Maria, both
working at demanding jobs, fight back. Maria recalls her life with
an ex-husband, "I left him dinner. It's called a can opener." Jokes
fly back and forth across the table, Eva's sons pulling baseball caps
on and off to swat their sides. I remember the first time I heard Eva
describe her family's sense of humor. Children who act out are
either "Los Talibanes" or "Al Qaeda," nicknames that make "the
termites" moniker for Chayo's grandchildren seem benign. Once,
Chana called on the other line while I was talking to Eva. "Pan-
zachita [big belly]," Eva greeted her. Dark humor, sprung from
fierce love. Now, Eva suppresses a grin as her daughters stand their
ground, their brothers' jests a thin veneer over pride in their sisters'
accomplishments.

Chana, recently promoted to a supervisory position at Wells
Fargo Bank, tells the story of a local customer whom she helped
with a recent transaction. When they finished, he said, "How did
a little Mexican girl like you grow up to be so smart?" In the face
of the racism Eva has fought her entire life, Chana simply stood
straight and said, "My mother raised me to always do the best
I can." The story hangs in the humid air. I glance at Eva's face,
illuminated now. She has given her life to nurturing this: Chana's
ability to rise above racism; Maria's gratitude for a child whose
health demands constant attention; Ralph's devotion to his grandchildren as his own; Marty's recovery from war wounds to serve
young people in his community; Ricky's dedication to his wife,

children, and home; Diego's stature as a community leader, family man, and surrogate father to his siblings; Chayo's commitment to teaching as well as family life; Cami's generous spirit as the man those in need "wait for."

The sky darkens with storm clouds over the low, broad onion fields. Before we return to the Best Western in Ontario, Eva gives us tortillas and sweet breads wrapped in hand-embroidered towels. This is an *itacate*, provisions for a journey bundled and knotted "just the way you would wrap a baby to take to the fields." As Eva anticipates the move into her shimmering new house, she never forgets that she came from "the onions."

"Next time," she promises as we get into the car, "you can stay here!"

"When do you think you'll move in?" I ask.

She just smiles and shrugs. For all of her keen appreciation for beauty and love of bargain treasures, they matter little. Loss of a house or anything in the physical world may dampen but cannot defeat the spirit. Inventive people will always create anew. Eva learned this from her parents, *artesanos* who forged beauty from the natural world and from scraps from the dump. La Casa is everything; La Casa is nothing.

Epilogue: My Spiritual Legs

La Enfermedad: Life has hurt sometimes
very, very deeply. Big, big, thick scars.

El Remedio: But they [the scars] taught me. Do
not regret. I need to feel the pain in order to go
forward and help others. Like my daddy says, "Stand
straight. Go through it as fast as you can. By the
time you reach the other end, you will know a lot."

ON A BRIGHT APRIL DAY, I search for buds on the rosebush outside Eva's back door. What I really long to see is the hummingbird that hovers over the blossoms in late spring and summer. But Bob and I have come too early for this harbinger of good luck. Predictions of abundance, Eva has taught me, are not simple or untouched by darkness. She once said, "In spring, my roses will bloom, but I won't know them until they have scratched my arm." Pain is so often wed to joy in Eva's life.

We visit in the casita, watching Mexican television. Eva has lost weight since I last saw her; she pauses between breaths as she speaks. A car pulls into the driveway—a woman arrives to be healed. I imagine the energy this encounter will demand of Eva. From the moment she kneels to massage someone's feet through the diagnosis and treatment, she attends fully to the person before her—in her words, "the God I wait for." "Do you feel up to this today?" I ask. "These legs are weak," she says, pointing to her beige drawstring pants, "but my spiritual legs are strong."

Bob and I linger in the kitchen as Eva carries a jar of herbs to the front room, where the heavy, raven-haired woman waits. Her face creases with worry; dark shadows circle her eyes. As Eva takes her hands, the woman begins to relax, her body sagging into a chair. I have long witnessed Eva's generosity as a healer; equally often, I've seen her deny her own multiple forms of pain. Some ills are physical. The disease she will not name remains in remission, but the threat of another stroke lingers. Arthritis decreases her fingers' dexterity. Earlier, she gripped the "y" between her thumb and forefinger with her other hand, as though to press out the dull ache. "I can't do the *azahares* anymore, Jo," she said of her inability to bend fingers around the tiniest orange blossoms for her *coronas*. But Eva doesn't linger on naming an illness; she simply moves past it. "I called Cami in Texas and asked him to get some *azahares* from Matamoros when he goes over to see his uncle."

Spiritual heaviness is the healer's burden. Added to the ailments individuals bring to her, Eva's work with troubled young people and their families grows more taxing each year. The health department condemned the trailer on Nyssa's edge that housed her Youth on the Move program. Dust clings to the Virgin of Guadalupe on one wall; a portion of the ceiling caves inward, bent by water that threatens the electrical lines. The toilet is perpetually clogged, its pipes intertwined with the roots of the towering trees outside. Eva now works with the kids in their homes, but driving tires her. She wants to reinhabit the trailer, but it will take money. Meanwhile, drive-by shootings in nearby Fruitland and in Nyssa have shaken these communities. "But there is nothing for the kids to do!" Eva laments. She relates the latest tales of escalating family violence, adding that the daily demands sometimes overwhelm her. "I see the word 'life' flash before me, and I feel nauseated," she says.

I'm worried as I go out to the car to get a notebook. When I reenter the casita, the visitor dons her jacket to leave. She smiles, lines crinkling around her eyes, the tautness released from her face. Eva looks renewed, too, as though the gift has replenished giver as well as receiver. Eva's usual good spirits resurface as she describes to Bob how she puts on her "Jesus glasses" when she wakes up. "It helps me see the world the way Jesus would see the world." Her Jesus glasses are bifocal, for they also offer a view of divinity in others. "It's easy to love that Jesus in the picture on the wall," Eva says. "He doesn't talk back. He's not going to kick me. He's been gone for two thousand years." She thinks for a minute, then in characteristic Eva fashion says, "But they said it was two thousand when I was growing up. They need to change that timing! Anyway, it's harder to love the Jesus in front of me. He or she might be difficult. They might not listen. But that's the Jesus I'm interested in."

I remember a day many years ago when I asked Eva how she would characterize her life. "A beautiful patchwork," she said. "Do not regret. I do not regret anything that has happened. Life has hurt sometimes very, very deeply. Big, big, thick scars. But they taught me." After Angie's death, some of her friends urged her to take antidepressants. But she is adamant that she doesn't want "happy pills." "I need to feel the pain in order to go forward and help others."

Throughout the casita are reminders of Eva's scars and of the accompanying lessons: family photos that include children and grandchildren who have died, the special stick that spoke to her at a time of spiritual doubt. That stick has a sibling Eva keeps in her car. Many years ago, Eva had a flat tire out on the highway close to a river. She called Ted for a ride, then perched above the rushing water to wait. "I saw this piece of wood. The current kept smashing it against a rock wall. It would come back, and then get thrown against the wall again. I kept watching it. How weird, you know, it's just a stick so it can't get mad. It can't get sad, it can't get anything, but it could have holes or gashes or slashes. But it didn't. It was so smooth, even being thrown back and forth by forceful water. I went and got it and saved it. It's in the trunk of my car. Whenever I feel that I'm going to be bitter, I go and look at it. Like my Daddy says, 'Stand straight. Go through it as fast as you can. By the time you reach the other end, you will know a lot.'"

As we gather our belongings to leave, I reflect on the stick—battered yet not disfigured. Eva's deep commitment to life always revitalizes me. One source of renewal is the story Eva told during our visit to the Fishtrap House in Enterprise for Day of the Dead in 2002. I think back to this tale of the rich man's quest for miracles, exposed by the master as futile because the man could muster no awe at the daily sunrise. The morning after Eva's talk, I woke in our B&B to the usual gray Oregon skies. My spirits were deflated; I pined for sun through the russet trees outside my window. But in the distance, light emanated from deep under the clouds. On days that seem bleak, I hear Eva's voice. "I believe in the sun, even if it's cloudy and I can't see it. I know it's there. You have a choice every day about how to live."

I've discovered other stories about the sunrise, including one that comes from Eva's indigenous heritage. The Aztec god of the sun is often depicted as a hummingbird, Huitzilopochtli. The story mixes history with legend. The hummingbird led the Mexica people into the central Valley of Mexico from Aztlán, the "place of whiteness," toward a new home, pausing at Coatepec, "Snake Mountain." There, the hummingbird god rose up from the earth as the sun destined to be reborn anew each day.[1]

I like the dreamy quality of this sunrise story. But I never forget its contradictions, for Huitzilopochtli was also the god of war, who spilled blood to nourish the "heavenly body 'which makes the day.'"[2] For the Aztecs, this duality was the knotty source of truth, poetry, its ultimate expression.

In my office, these gifts from Eva line the shelves and walls:

A hummingbird cup

A white clay bowl with hummingbirds circling the sides

A tiny hummingbird teetering inside a small circle of tin

A sky-blue wall-hanging filled with hummingbirds

A towel with luminous green hummingbirds

A hummingbird dashboard ornament with a stick-on bottom

And the belief that luck may alight on my shoulders

And when it does not, when times are darkest, I go to Eva for faith, the way she goes to the Pregnant Earth to root herself in its sage and copper sustenance. When I feel alone, she reminds me that our truest selves emerge when we loosen individual boundaries and bleed into a community. Pain is inescapable: "Although it

be jade, it will be broken/although it be gold, it will be crushed."
But alongside suffering, the daily miracle. The meaning of this
duality may come to us only fleetingly, a brief transcendence. Some
call this God; others find it more elusive, resistant to our naming. Glimpses may come through metaphor, like so many of Eva's
truths. These metaphors carry us over—even momentarily—the
gaps and schisms in our broken world, offering a path toward
healing.

NOTES

PREFACE

1. I use the feminine *curandera* throughout most of the book to avoid the awkward o/a form and because much of the research cited focuses on women healers.

2. *Flor y canto* is often described as the first poetry of the Americas. See Alison Hawthorne Deming, ed., *The Poetry of the American West* (New York: Columbia University Press, 1996), 1–8. The quote about jade and gold is attributed to King Nezahualcóyotl in *The Colección Cantares Mexicanos* fol. 2, ed. Antonio Peñafiel, cited in León-Portilla's *Aztec Thought and Culture: A Study of the Ancient Nahuatl Mind* (Norman: University of Oklahoma Press, 1963), 5.

INTRODUCTION

1. The choice among the terms "Chicano" or "Latino" or "Hispanic" for Spanish-speaking North Americans and their descendants continues to inspire debate. The U.S. Census Bureau uses "Hispanic" and "Latino" interchangeably. "Chicano" refers to the political/social-rights movement begun in the 1960s and '70s. "Latino" often connotes ties to an Indo-American rather than a Spanish heritage. Activists and scholars began to use "Latino" in the 1970s to reflect "an anti-assimilationist" political

consciousness. I use the term "Latina/Latino" throughout, as it seems most inclusive; occasionally, I substitute "Chicano" to stress the political dimension. See Suzanne Oboler, *Ethnic Labels, Latino Lives: Identity and the Politics of (Re)presentation in the United States* (Minneapolis, Minn: University of Minnesota Press, 1995); and Latina Feminist Group, "Introduction: *Papelitos Guardados*; Theorizing *Latinidades* through *Testimonio*," in *Telling to Live: Latina Feminist Testimonios* (Durham, NC: Duke University Press, 2001), 1–24.

2. The National Endowment for the Arts initiated the National Heritage Awards in 1982 to honor culturally diverse traditional artists in the United States. For more information, see www.nea.gov/honors/heritage/index.html.

3. This is the opening line of *I Rigoberta Menchú: An Indian Woman in Guatemala*, ed. Elisabeth Burgos-Debray, trans. Ann Wright (London: Verso, 1984). For a discussion of the importance of *testimonio* as a narrative form, see Latina Feminist Group, *Telling to Live*, 1–24. For a *testimonio* that alternates between a novelistic storytelling style and oral tradition, see Ruth Behar, *Translated Woman: Crossing the Border with Esperanza's Story* (Boston: Beacon Press, 1993).

1. MEASURING FAITH

1. One of Mexico's oldest indigenous groups, the Otomí was one of several that occupied the northern and eastern borders of the Aztec and Tarascan empires at the time of the Spanish conquest in the 1500s. For readers interested in the heritage of the Otomí in Mexico, see James Dow, *The Otomí of the Northern Sierra de Puebla, Mexico: An Ethnographic Outline*, Monograph Series no. 12 (East Lansing: Latin American Studies Center, Michigan State University, June 1975). For a discussion of ongoing Otomí customs, see Phyllis M. Correa, "Otomí Rituals and Celebrations: Crosses, Ancestors, and Resurrection," *Journal of American Folklore* 113, no. 450 (Autumn 2000): 436–50.

2. I use "Aztec" rather than "Mexica" throughout the book, since this

is the term Eva uses for her father's heritage. For 150 years before Spanish colonization, the Aztecs dominated the political and social life of the Nahuatl-speaking groups (Nahua) that inhabited the central valley of Mexico. Nahuatl is the most widely spread of the Uto-Azteca language family. See Earl Shorris, *The Life and Times of Mexico* (New York: Norton, 2004) 7–8; and León-Portilla, *Aztec Thought and Culture*, xvii–xix.

2. THE STORY TOO BIG TO TELL

1. For a fuller discussion of Las Siete Luminarias, see Oscar Jesús Cortés Toledo, *La Monografía de Valle de Santiago* Gto. 2 Edición (privately printed: Valle de Santiago, Guanajuato, Mexico, n.d.), 90–103.

2. Being "stolen" before a wedding is a ritual still practiced in some parts of Mexico. A bride is "deposited" at the home of relatives before the wedding. For a fuller discussion, see chapter 7.

3. David E. Lorey, *The U.S.–Mexican Border in the Twentieth Century* (Wilmington, DE: Scholarly Resources, 1999), 56–63.

4. For a psychological view of fairy tales and folktales, see Bruno Bettelheim, *The Uses of Enchantment* (New York: Vintage, 1989). For other theoretical perspectives and an overview, see Jack Zipes, *Why Fairy Tales Stick: The Evolution and Relevance of a Genre* (New York: Routledge, 1996).

5. Ted Chamberlin, *If This Is Your Land, Where Are Your Stories?* (Toronto: Alfred A. Knopf Canada, 2003), 238.

3. CROSSING OVER

1. Américo Paredes coined the term "Greater Mexico" for the border region as well as for Mexican culture in a broad sense, beyond geographic residence. See *With a Pistol in His Hand: A Border Ballad and Its Hero* (Austin: University of Texas Press, 1958). José Limón elaborated the use of the term. See *American Encounters* (Boston: Beacon Press, 1998). For an over-

view of Mexican South Texas as a distinct geographic and cultural region, see Daniel D. Arreola, *Tejano South Texas: A Mexican American Province* (Austin: University of Texas Press, 2002); and Lorey, *The U.S.–Mexican Border in the Twentieth Century.*

2. William Langewiesche, *Cutting for Sign* (New York: Pantheon, 1993), 44.

3. David Montejano, *Anglos and Mexicans in the Making of Texas, 1836–1986* (Austin: University of Texas Press, 1987).

4. For an overview of United States–Mexico labor relations in the first half of the twentieth century, see Rodolfo Acuña, *Occupied America: A History of Chicanos* (New York: Harper and Row, 1981), 121–51.

5. Erasmo Gamboa, "The Bracero Program," in *Nosotros: The Hispanic People of Oregon*, ed. Erasmo Gamboa and Carolyn M. Baun (Portland: Oregon Council for the Humanities, 1995), 41–44.

6. Acuña, *Occupied America*, 284.

7. Ned Wallace, "The 1971 Pharr Riot," in *Studies in Rio Grande Valley History*, UTB/TSC Regional History Series 6, ed. Milo Kearney, Anthony Knopp, and Antonio Zavaleta (Brownsville: University of Texas, 2005), 17–39.

8. For an overview of the Chicano labor movement on farms and in factories, see Acuña, *Occupied America*, 284–90

9. Hector Tobar, "Mexicans Put Own Mask on Halloween," *Los Angeles Times*, October 31, 2007.

10. See Stanley Brandes, *Skulls to the Living, Bread to the Dead: The Day of the Dead in Mexico and Beyond* (Malden, MA: Blackwell, 2006), 133–53; and George Acona, *Pablo Remembers: The Fiesta of the Day of the Dead* (New York: Harper Collins, 1993).

11. Cynthia Ozick, "Toward a New Yiddish" in *Art and Ardor* (New York: Knopf, 1983), 154.

12. Nancy Venable Raine, *After Silence: Rape and My Journey Back* (New York: Three Rivers Press, 1998), 163.

4. *LA MULA*

1. Elizabeth D. de la Portilla writes, "Though crying in the womb is physiologically impossible, it is believed that the mother can feel her child sob." See "San Antonio as Magical Crossroads: Healing and Spirituality on the Borderlands" (PhD dissertation, Department of Anthropology, University of Michigan, 2002), 93.

2. Inés Hernández Ávila, "Dispelling the Sombras: Grito mi nombre con rayos de luz," in *Telling to Live: Latina Feminist Testimonios*, 239.

3. Edén E. Torres stresses this link between individual and collective trauma. See "Anguished Past, Troubled Present," in *Chicana without Apology: Chicana sin Vergüenza: The New Chicana Cultural Studies* (New York: Routledge, 2003), 11–46. Fran Leeper Buss offers an excellent overview of the contexts of male violence and also cautions against stereotyping Mexican men as "macho" in her introduction to *Forged under the Sun/Forjada bajo el sol: The Life of Maria Elena Lucas* (Ann Arbor: University of Michigan Press, 1993), 24–26.

5. THE DRESS THAT DOESN'T FIT

1. Deming, *The Poetry of the American West*, 2.

2. Migration to the United States has played a role in furthering evangelism, with returning migrants bringing U.S. evangelical practices with them. See Jeremy Schwartz, "Evangelical Influence Growing," *Miami Herald*, March 27, 2005; and Adelle M. Banks, "Latinos Bringing New Vigor to Religious Landscape in U.S.," *Oregonian*, April 26, 2007, A4. For a look at how Pentecostal churches aid communities, see Fernanda Santos, "A Populist Threat Confronts the Catholic Church," *New York Times*, April 20, 2008, 30.

3. Moises Sandoval, *On the Move: A History of the Hispanic Church in the United States* (New York: Orbis, 1990).

4. Gabriella Ricciardi, "Telling Stories, Building Altars: Mexican American Women's Altars in Oregon," *Oregon Historical Quarterly* 107, no. 4 (Winter 2006): 536–52.

5. Eric Wolf analyzes the Virgin of Guadalupe as symbol in "The Virgin of Guadalupe: A Mexican National Symbol," in *Pathways of Power: Building an Anthropology of the Modern World*, ed. Eric Wolf, with Sydel Silverman (Berkeley: University of California Press, 2001), 139–46. For a discussion of the meaning of the Virgin in women's lives, see Jeanette Rodriguez, *Our Lady of Guadalupe: Faith and Empowerment among Mexican American Women* (Austin: University of Texas Press, 1994).

6. León-Portilla, *Aztec Thought and Culture*, 183.

7. Erasmo Gamboa, "El Movimiento: Oregon's Mexican-American Civil Rights Movement," in *Nosotros: The Hispanic People of Oregon*, 48–49.

8. For more on the family system in Mexican American communities, see Norma Williams, *The Mexican American Family: Tradition and Change* (Dix Hills, NY: General Hall, 1990).

6. Choosing Ripeness

1. See Norma E. Cantú, "La Quinceañera: Toward an Ethnographic Analysis of a Life Cycle Ritual," *Southern Folklore* 56, no. 1 (1999), 73–101 and "Chicana Life-Cycle Rituals," in *Chicana Traditions: Continuity and Change*, ed. Norma E. Cantú and Olga Nájera-Ramírez (Urbana: University of Illinois Press, 2002), 15–34.

2. Julia Alvarez, *Once Upon a Quinceañera: Coming of Age in the U.S.A.* (New York: Penguin, 2007), 121.

3. Ibid, 223–27.

4. Vicki Ruiz, *From Out of the Shadows: Mexican Women in Twentieth-Century America* (New York: Oxford University Press, 1998), 105.

5. See Ruiz, 106–07 for an analysis of Malinche.

6. For overviews of Latina feminism, see Gloria Anzaldúa, *Making Face, Making Soul/Haciendo Caras: Creative and Critical Perspectives by Feminists of Color* (San Francisco: Spinsters/Aunt Lute Books, 1990); Alma Garcia, *Chicana Feminist Thought: The Basic Historical Writings* (New York: Routledge, 1997); Latina Feminist Group, *Telling to Live*; Carla Trujillo, ed., *Living Chicana Theory* (Berkeley: Third Woman Press, 1998); Adela de la Torre and Beatríz M. Pesquera, eds., *Building with Our Hands: New Directions in Chicana Studies* (Berkeley: University of California Press, 1993); and Vicki Ruiz, "La Nueva Chicana: Women and the Movement," in *From Out of the Shadows*, 99–126; Denise A. Segura and Beatriz M. Pesquera, "Chicana Feminisms: Their Political Context and Contemporary Feminisms," in *The Latino Studies Reader*, ed. Antonia Darder and Rodolfo D. Torres (Malden, MA: Blackwell, 1998), 193–205.

7. Audre Lorde, "The Master's Tools Will Never Dismantle the Master's House" in *Sister Outsider: Essays and Speeches* (Berkeley: Crossing Press, 1984), 110–13.

7. GNAWING THE BONE

1. Inga Clendinnen, *Aztecs: An Interpretation* (New York: Cambridge University Press, 1955), 161.

2. Jennifer S. Hirsch, *A Courtship after Marriage: Sexuality and Love in Mexican Transnational Families* (Berkeley: University of California Press, 2003), 87–88, 90–91.

3. The Spanish legal code divided rape into three categories. *Rapto* meant the daughter was seen as a willing partner in her flight from the parents'

home to force their approval of a marriage; *estrupo*, from Roman law, was the "sexual use of an unmarried free person"; and *violación* referred to "forced sex." The last two categories often merged and only refer to "honest women," writes Sonya Lipsett-Rivera. See "The Intersection of Rape and Marriage in Late-Colonial and Early-National Mexico," *Colonial Latin American Historical Review* 6, no. 4 (Fall 1997), 563–90.

8. THE DOOR AND THE HINGE

1. Erasmo Gamboa, "El Movimiento: Oregon's Mexican-American Civil Rights Movement," in *Nosotros: The Hispanic People of Oregon*, 48.

9. THE CALL

1. Several sources look at the cross-cultural pattern of women being "called" and the ways that healing offers women power otherwise denied them. See Laurel Kendall, "Old Ghosts and Grateful Children: A Korean Shaman's Story," in *Women as Healers: Cross-Cultural Perspectives*, ed. Carol Shepherd McClain (New Brunswick, NJ: Rutgers University Press, 1989), 138–56. The volume as a whole gives a good overview of women healers.

2. Lewis Hyde, *The Gift* (New York: Vintage, 1979).

3. For a discussion of the community's acknowledgement of a *curandera*'s calling, see de la Portilla "San Antonio as Magical Crossroads," 25–26. De la Portilla and other scholars see gender as a critical factor in the practice and study of *curanderismo*. See also Françoise Verges, "Mind and Body: Revising Approaches to the Analysis of *Curanderismo*," in *Wings of Gauze: Women of Color and the Experience of Health and Illness*, ed. Barbara Bair and Susan E. Cayleff (Detroit: Wayne State University Press, 1993), 109–21.

4. Robert T. Trotter II and Juan Antonio Chavira, *Curanderismo: Mexican Folk Healing*, 2nd ed. (Athens: University of Georgia, 1997), 27; for the history of *curanderismo*, see chapter 2, 25–40.

5. de la Portilla, "San Antonio as Magical Crossroads," 48.

6. Elena Avila, *Woman Who Glows in the Dark* (New York: Jeremy P. Tarcher/Penguin Books, 1999), 22–24.

7. Guillermo Bonfil Batalla, *México Profundo: Reclaiming a Civilization*, trans. Philip A. Dennis (Austin: University of Texas Press, 1996).

8. de la Portilla, "San Antonio as Magical Crossroads," 71.

9. Torres, *Chicana without Apology: Chicana sin Vergüenza*, 154.

10. MAGICAL THINKING

1. Avila, *Woman Who Glows in the Dark*, 19.

2. Douglas Uzzell gives an overview of *susto* as escape from social pressures in "Susto Revisited: Illness as Strategic Role," *American Ethnologist* 1, no. 2 (Spring 1974): 369–78. See also Arthur J. Rubel and Carol W. O'Nell, "Difficulties of Presenting Complaints to Physicians: Susto Illness as an Example," in *Modern Medicine and Medical Anthropology in the United States-Mexico Border Population*, Publication no. 359, ed. Boris Velimirovic (Washington DC: Pan American Health Organization, 1978).

3. *Mal de ojo* and other illnesses are topics of extensive discussion in anthropological literature. See Robert T. Trotter II, "A Survey of Four Illnesses and Their Relationship to Intracultural Variation in a Mexican-American Community," *American Anthropologist*, New Series 93, no. 1 (March 1991): 115–25.

4. For more on *brujeria*, see Trotter and Chavira, *Curanderismo*, 31–32.

5. See Trotter and Chavira, *Curanderismo*, 1–24, for a summary of *curanderismo*. For an overview of the cultural construction of illness, see Arthur Kleinman, *Patients and Healers in the Context of Culture: An Explora-*

tion of the Borderland between Anthropology, Medicine, and Psychiatry
(Berkeley: University of California Press, 1980).

6. For a feminist critique of studies that analyze *curanderas* as conservative,
see Verges, "Mind and Body," 109–21.

7. An early and important article on healing is Arthur M. Kleinman,
"Medicine's Symbolic Reality: On a Central Problem in the Philosophy
of Medicine," *Inquiry* 16 (1973): 206–13. For a discussion of efficacy, see
James B. Waldram, "The Efficacy of Traditional Medicine: Current Theoretical and Methodological Issues," *Medical Anthropology Quarterly*,
"Theme Issue: Ritual Healing in Navajo Society," New Series 14, no. 4
(2000): 603–25.

8. Anne Harrington, *The Cure Within: A History of Mind-Body Medicine*
(New York: Norton, 2008), 18.

9. David Rieff, "Miracle Workers?" *New York Times Magazine* (February
17, 2008): 13–14.

10. Trotter and Chavira, *Curanderismo,* 67

11. "Imitative magic" forms part of a widely shared set of folk theories
about illness and cures. These include 1) imitative and contagious magic,
2) the intrusion of a disease-causing object, 3) soul loss, 4) spirit possession, and 5) breach of taboo. See John A. Hostetler, "Folk Medicine and
Sympathy Healing Among the Amish" in *American Folk Medicine: A Sym-
posium,* ed. Wayland D. Hand (Berkeley: University of California Press,
1976), 249–58.

12. See Victor Turner's treatment of symbols in *The Ritual Process* (Chicago: Aldine, 1969).

13. de la Portilla, "San Antonio as Magical Crossroads," 147

11. DRINKING IN THE PAIN

1. See León-Portilla, *Aztec Thought and Culture*, 119 – 22, for a discussion of self-control, free will, and fatalism.

2. The poem is translated from *Colleción de Cantares Mexicanos*, ed. Antonio Peñafiel, fol. 35, and cited in *Aztec Thought and Culture*, 131.

3. Octavio Paz, *The Labyrinth of Solitude* (New York: Grove, 1961), 57.

4. Stanley Brandes, "Is There a Mexican View of Death?" *Ethos* 31, no. 1 (2003):127–44.

5. Brandes, *Skulls to the Living, Bread to the Dead,* 181.

6. The Montaigne quote appears in Frank Graziano's *Cultures of Devotion: Folk Saints of Spanish America* (New York: Oxford University Press, 2007), 99. Chapter 2, "San La Muerte," traces the emergence and history of the folk saint, particularly in Argentina (77–111).

7. Ibid., 77–79.

8. For a description of pesticide use in Oregon, see "The Oregon Story: Oregon Farmworker Issues," aired by Oregon Public Broadcasting in 2001, www.opb.org/programs/oregonstory/ag_workers/issues.html.

12. CUTTING THE ONIONS

1. Jim Scutt, "CPOs Assessed in Law Enforcement and Victim Assistance: Improving Victim Services," cited in Teri Ottens, "Angie's Story: An Investigative Review of the Murder of Maria Evangelina 'Angie' Castellanoz Leon in Canyon County, May 19, 2003" (prepared by a task force of concerned citizens, May 19, 2004). All details of Angie's murder are taken from "Angie's Story."

2. Telephone conversation with Teri Ottens, October 11, 2005.

3. See the fact sheet of the National Latino Alliance for the Elimination of Domestic Violence at www.dvalianza.org/resor/factsheet_dv.htm.

13. THE MEXICAN JACUZZI

1. Thomas Lux, "Refrigerator, 1957," from *New and Selected Poems of Thomas Lux: 1975–1995* (New York: Houghton Mifflin, 1997), 4.

2. George Lakoff and Mark Johnson, *Metaphors We Live By* (Chicago: University of Chicago Press, 1980), 3–9.

3. Paul Stoller, "The Epistemology of Sorkotarey: Language, Metaphor and Healing among the Songhay," *Ethos* 8, no. 2 (1980): 117–31. For a more general view, see James W. Fernandez's analysis of the ritual actualization of metaphor in "The Performance of Ritual Metaphors," in *The Social Use of Metaphor: Essays on the Anthropology of Rhetoric*, ed. J. David Sapir and J. Christopher Crocker (Philadelphia: University of Pennsylvania Press, 1977), 100–131.

4. The description of the wise men is from *Códice Matritense de la Real Academia de la Historia* (Nahuatl texts of the Indian informants of Fray Bernardino de Sahagún), Facsimile ed. of Vol. VIII by Francisco del Paso y Troncoso (Madrid, Hauser y Menet, 1907), the last lines of fol. 118 r. and the first half of fol. 118 v. cited in León-Portilla, *Aztec Thought and Culture*, 11. The link between poetry and scientific knowledge appears on page 16.

5. In *Aztec Thought and Culture*, León-Portilla describes how Nahuatl poetry—*In xóchitl in cuícatl—flor y canto* (flower and song)—rests on *difrasismo*, the expression of a single idea by two words that function as a metaphor, a stylistic trait of the Nahuatl language, 102–3. León-Portilla also discusses *diafrasismo* in *Fifteen Poets of the Aztec World* (Norman: University of Oklahoma Press, 1992), 54.

6. Susan Sontag, *Illness as Metaphor* (New York: Farrar, Strauss and Giroux, 1978). Raymond W. Gibbs and Heather Franks analyze the use of metaphor among cancer patients in "Embodied Metaphors in Women's Narratives about their Experience with Cancer," *Health Communication* 14, no. 2 (2002): 139–65.

7. Laurence J. Kirmayer, "Healing and the Invention of Metaphor: The Effectiveness of Symbols Revisited," *Culture, Medicine and Psychiatry* 17, no. 2 (1993): 162.

8. Northrop Frye cites Baudelaire's description of a poem's "suggestive magic" as well as Wallace Steven's notion that the motive for metaphor is the "desire to associate, and finally to identify, the human mind with what goes on outside it because the only genuine joy we can have is in those rare moments when you feel that although we know in part, as Paul says, we are also a part of what we know." See Northrop Frye, "The Motive for Metaphor," in *The Norton Reader*, 8th ed. (New York: Norton, 1992), 1055–63.

14. MY PIECE OF THE PUZZLE

1. For a fuller version of this local history, see "Nyssa" in Malheur County History (Malheur County, OR: Malheur County Historical Society, 1988), 97–103. The 1911 brochure is cited on the website of the Oregon Historical Society's Oregon History Project, www.ohs.org/education/oregonhistory/historical_records/dspDocument.cfm? doc_ID=0008EEDA-669E-1E35-925B80B05272006C.

2. Diego Castellanoz is one of the people interviewed for the Stories Project of the Citizens Trade Campaign Fair Trade, www.citizenstrade.org/interviews/.

3. "The Oregon Story: Who Are the Workers?" Oregon Public Broadcasting, www.opb.org/programs/oregonstory/ag_workers/issues.html.

4. Alma M. Garcia, *Narratives of Mexican American Women: Emergent*

Identities of the Second Generation (Walnut Creek, CA: AltaMira Press, 2004).

15. Ask Me

1. In the 1990's, Oregon high schools began to require students to earn a Certificate of Initial Mastery (CIM) to meet Oregon's performance standards in different disciplines. The CIM was phased out in 2008. For more information, see the "Standards" and "Certificate of Initial Mastery" Topics at: www.ode.state.or.us. Also see http://oregon.schooltree.org/public/Nyssa-High. The federal No Child Left Behind Act (Public Law 107-110) was signed on January 8, 2002, requiring students to meet certain test-based standards.

2. Bill Bigelow, Brenda Harvey, Stan Karp, and Larry Miller, "Failing Our Kids: What's Wrong with the Testing Craze" in *Rethinking Our Classrooms, Volume 2: Teaching for Equity and Justice* (Milwaukee, WI: Rethinking Schools, 2001), 204–206.

3. The Latino youth dropout rate was more than three times greater than the 2000 non-Hispanic Caucasian dropout rate of 6.9 percent. See www.ericdigests.org/2004-3/latino.html (Educational Research and Improvement Center document of the U.S. Government). For discussion of the cycle of low expectations and student behavior, see J. Abi-nader, "A House for My Mother: Motivating Hispanic High School Students," *Anthropology and Education Quarterly* 21, no. 3 (1990): 41–58.

4. Denise A. Segura, "Slipping through the Cracks," in *Building with Our Hands: New Directions in Chicano Studies*, ed. Adela de la Torre and Beatríz M. Pesquera (Berkeley: University of California Press, 1993), 199–216.

5. Quotes from Grotting, Bates, and other school officials are excerpted from Jay Hutchins, "Rocking the Boat in Mountain Time: Nyssa School

District," an interview with Nyssa School District officials in *Oregon's Future* 6, no. 2 (Summer 2005): 18–22.

6. Phone conversation with Luke Newton, December 10, 2008.

16. REVIVING THE ROOT

1. Avelardo Valdez, "Toward a Typology of Contemporary Mexican American Youth Gangs," in *Gangs and Society*, ed. Louis Kontos, David Brotherton, and Luis Barrios (New York: Columbia University Press, 2003), 12–40.

2. Luis Barrios, "The Almighty Latin King and Queen Nation and the Spirituality of Resistance: Agency, Social Cohesion, and Liberating Rituals in the Making of a Street Organization," in *Gangs and Society*, 120.

3. Ibid., 183. The quote is from Queen H.

4. Tom Hayden, *Street Wars: Gangs and the Future of Violence* (New York: New Press, 2004), 86.

17. HEALING WOMEN

1. From Idaho News Channel KTVB, report by Andrea Dearden, "Abel Leon Gets Life Sentence for Killing His Wife," Friday, October 1, 2004.

18. A COURAGEOUS HEART

1. Norman R. Heitzman Jr., "A Force Overlooked: Achieving Full Representation of Hispanics in the Department of Defense Workforce," (Washington, DC: National Council of La Raza, 1999), www.nclr.org/content/news/detail/2169.

2. Jorge Mariscal, "They Only Call Us Americans When They Need Us for War: The Paradox of Mexican-Americans at War," *Counterpunch* (June

24, 2005). See also Ralph Guzman, "Mexican-American Casualties in Vietnam," *La Raza* 1, no. 1 (1970): 12–15.

3. "Latinos and the War in Iraq," Pew Hispanic Center, http://pew hispanic.org/files/factsheets/27.pdf.

EPILOGUE: MY SPIRITUAL LEGS

1. Clendinnen, *Aztecs: An Interpretation*, 22.

2. León-Portilla, *Aztec Thought and Culture*, 161.